CORBIN BOSILJEVAC

On to the Next Thing

A Memoir on Crime, Choices and Change

First published by Blu Press Media 2021

Library of Congress Control Number: 2021907259

It is the intent for the content in this book to be used as inspiration, information, and advice based on the personal experiences of one man. The reader should not consider the words herein to be advice from a medical, counseling, or psychological professional. It can, however, be viewed as solid life events in which to draw wisdom from. Enjoy!

First edition

ISBN: 978-1-7357217-3-6

Editing by Dr. Joseph Bosiljevac
Cover art by Liliana Guia
Advisor: Kalia Keosybounheuang
Editing by Pamela Humphreys

This book was professionally typeset on Reedsy.
Find out more at reedsy.com

In time, I realized that facing my fears and living in the world was the only solution that made sense. I now pray that the world continues in the direction of acceptance and understanding while empowering individuals toward their inherent right of freedom.

Contents

Foreword

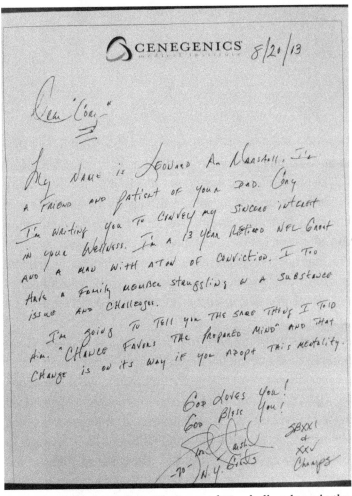

CENEGENICS 8/20/13

Dear "Cory"

My Name is Leonard An Marshall. I'm a friend and patient of your Dad. Cory I'm writing you to convey my sincere interest in your Wellness. I'm a 13 year Retired NFL Great and a man with a ton of conviction. I too have a family member struggling w a substance issue and challenges.

I'm going to tell you the same thing I told him. "Chance favors the prepared mind" and that change is on its way if you adopt this mentality.

God loves you!
God bless you!

Len Marshall
-70- N.Y. Giants
SBXXI
&
XXV
Champs

An encouraging letter from Mr. Leonard Marshall early on in the prison sentence.

Preface

There are people we talk to every day who would confess that their lives may not have turned out as they intended. Most will freely admit that events such and finding love, changing professions, or dealing with health issues all shape the plot line in each of our individual stories. Usually, our upbringing and education build a foundation that carries us through a life that may not go as planned but unfolds into one of the greatest and most unique journeys imaginable. We all have a story to tell. Some just take unexpected turns that don't necessarily correlate to how they began.

My life started out as normal as you can imagine; a robust middle-class upbringing in rural America that taught me to respect others, work hard, and appreciate what life hands us. Having a doctor as a father and a mother who involved herself in every aspect of her kids' lives afforded me numerous opportunities to enjoy my childhood and look forward to growing up strong and healthy. Excelling at high school sports, enjoying vacations with family, and graduating from the University of Kansas were all milestones in a line of happy achievements and vivid memories.

Then, over the course of several years, when I transitioned into the workforce as an outside salesman for a Fortune 1000 telecom company, I started making rash decisions. I made choices that led me down a path that was peculiar and contrary to my solid upbringing. It could be blamed on mental illness, addiction, social anxiety, or just plain greed. Either way, my choices over this time were out of character and began to change my life for the worse. I may have been searching for something, though I still cannot quite pinpoint what that something was. It could have been the undue pressure I put on myself to show success through worldly and materialistic measures.

The downward departure in my life did not happen overnight but over the course of five to six years. I started treating people differently, not respectfully or with humble engagement; it was more entitlement and expected want. I took to doing drugs more and drinking irresponsibly. Being successful in outside sales led to happy hours after work at the bar that would stretch into the wee hours of the morning without a care for the consequences. From working in the corporate world to learning how to navigate the streets in the shady dealings of illegal drugs isn't the typical progression for job advancement. It is, however, the path I took without a second thought to the dangers surrounding my activities. In these writings, you will hear about what haphazard decision-making and dauntless actions eventually earned me. You'll absorb from my perspective how careless undertakings and poor follow-through can bring devastating results without warning. Subsequently, you will see how determined resolve brought me back to prominence no matter how far I had fallen. Resilience is a beautiful thing.

I could have made excuses, if I wanted to, but I didn't. What kind of excuses would anyone have believed anyhow? Any pains or hardships were brought on by myself and my own actions. As artless as it may be, our choices are the essence of innumerable pains we go through in life. I didn't start with a clear direction or formula for composing this book, but it has been tremendously important for my own sanity and purpose that it be a depiction of my experiences, beliefs, stories, and lessons learned from the trials and tribulations I've overcome. I basically sat down over the course of many months to put ideas on paper in order to share them with you. Some segments portray by what means I figured out how to come out the other side of a fast-paced and roller-coaster version of a life that I led for many years. Hard and risky times gave way to spiritual awakenings and modest new beginnings for what is now a life I would have never planned for myself - but wouldn't trade for anything in the world.

"On to the next thing" is a phrase that we used in prison, specifically at the Leavenworth Prison Camp where I spent four of my six years in the federal system. This phrase was our way of keeping ourselves moving forward in the mundane existence we lived through each day. As long as we kept moving on to the next designated activity, planned or forced by the authority figures, then time would keep marching on and we would continue our prison sentences uninterrupted. It was a way to stay positive in a mostly dull and impeding environment; a place where none of us wanted to be but where assimilation was our only real choice. This ever-changing community was always on the edge of insanity and depression, but it was there where I confess that so much good came from this controlled setting. In that place there was the sharing of stories with fellow inmates and comradery with strangers in support of one another. The men I spent time with were all striving to reinvent themselves through the purpose of going back out into the world as better people equipped to take on life new and restored.

Yes, getting out of prison was just as hard as going in, though with a much brighter horizon to look forward to. From the invasion of my house by the SWAT team, to the renewal of a holiness that had long been forgotten, these accounts will prove that a person can change in huge ways. It starts with adaptation into a community structure so unfamiliar that it broke me to the core. It then leads to the hesitant joy of freedom once it finally arrives years later. I wouldn't wish these hardships on anyone, and yet I praise a God who pulled me through it all and now thank Him for the experiences it has left me.

I hope these stories that I share will resonate with you and help bring sympathy to those suffering a similar fate in the prison system. I also want to inspire hope in others who feel that falling short is part of their DNA that will forever define them. As long as you are breathing air, then there's a purpose and need for you in the world. Moving on to the next thing is all that you need to focus on.

I intended this to be a compilation that is entertaining and encouraging at the same time. It isn't an "against all odds" story where you are enamored by the protagonist and motivated to conquer the world after reading it. No, it's meant to hit you square between the eyes with a reality check. A reminder that we can all make bad choices at times and get caught up in the foibles of life. We also can make up for those shortcomings by simplifying our focus and living in the moment we are given.

Acknowledgement

Many hugs and kisses to my family who support me through all my hiccups and folly. Cheryl, Joven, TyBoss, Kpax, Gramsy, Janice and Lex, Tim and Sandi, Ron and Judy, Teri and Ron, Jacquelyn, Carol, Kaden, Karli, Addi, Maclin and B-Kay, Brook and Callie. Thank you to the communities who welcomed me back with open arms and love. Much gratitude to those who communicated with me throughout my prison sentence. Jerry and Dana, Cristian and Lisa, Q, Kess, Shaw, Geitz, Colt, Amye, Kelly, Chad, Mr. Leonard Marshall, Rand, Bob and Judy, Buck and Donna. Finally, thank you to my Lord Jesus Christ who truly did carry me through the times where I did not have the strength to walk on my own.

THE INCIDENT

"My life is like a speeding bullet
that just hasn't hit the target yet."
—Kid Cudi

They yelled, mocked, harassed, and altogether annoyed the ever-living shit out of me. I didn't even know I was being watched while I slowly mopped the dayroom floor. After being in jail for only a few days, I still wasn't aware that everything you do or say is judged by everyone else in there and any weaknesses observed are exposed for the sake of entertainment. It's just how things are when you are incarcerated. Inmates are bored and new fish are easy targets.

So, I yelled back at them, shaming them for caring about why I was dragging the mop the way I did. Who cares if I was slow or plodding and probably not doing a very thorough job? The floors needed cleaning, it was my day to clean them, and I was in no hurry to complete the task. What else was there to do in this place anyhow? I had no idea anybody would be watching or maneuvering against me. I was new, and naïve, and I didn't know how to handle the situation.

It ended up that I made things harder on myself by hollering at

1

them. They laughed and increased their insulting with vigor and excitement. I had fallen into their trap—the new guy having a rough time adjusting to the cramped quarters. I got pissed, all up in my emotions, heavy air in my chest with the swirling of yellow in my head. Now my feelings were out on display for these guys to mimic and flaunt. I thought, "Crap, I'm in over my head, and this sucks horribly."

Five seasoned inmates were gathered around driving me about my newness, my shoddy cleaning job, my shirt being compactly tucked in, and anything else that crossed their minds. It felt like high school, but these guys were serious and more convicted in their testing. My face felt red with embarrassment while my elbows began to quiver. While looking sideways I muttered to myself, "What the fuck is going on here?" Had I regressed into some primal ritual of hazing? Was I about to get my ass kicked? Should I take the beating or do the best I could to blast my way out of this escalating horror? I was confused by the terror of the unknown. Life in jail was getting off to a terrible start.

In an instant, one of the taller guys with a shaved head and swastika tattoo on his temple spun me around by my shoulder. He slapped me across the top of my head and stunned me with what he said next. "Let it wash over ya, man!" he blurted out. "Don't fight it, you gotta be in here whether ya like it or not." I stood there with a floppy look on my face as I realized what was going on. They were trying me out and, luckily, they took a liking to me. There weren't very many white guys in our pod, so they wanted to see what I was made of. How I "represented" so to say.

So, it began, the first initiation into my new life. I wasn't used to this sort of behavior and certainly wasn't prepared for these guys to take me under their protection. But it happened there *and so did the genesis of my schooling—how to handle myself around a bunch of guys who want to get underneath my skin.*

I didn't get bloodied that day, and I started to learn a lesson that was life-saving for me once I understood it years later. It had to do with taking your prison sentence like a man and keeping a sane mind in an insane existence. Letting the wave of your situation wash over you like the breakers of the ocean. Just let it happen and be strong.

I couldn't fight my own presence in prison; I just had to be there, in it with everyone else. When these guys first started to bug me that day, I thought I could brush them off and keep to myself. But that wasn't healthy, and they were only doing what they did every other day in that place. Once I understood these concepts, then I could cope with the reality of my situation. It didn't happen quickly, but I worked on it and it helped. It helped me move on to the next thing.

Pulling into my neighbor's driveway and parking behind her car didn't seem like a problem that night. It was after ten in the evening, and I would be stopping home for only a few minutes. This would be enough time to gather the pills I needed for the next transaction. I had been on my usual route for a weekday, and it was now creeping into the evening hours. After dealing drugs for several years, I had established loyal customers, good soldiers that helped me move my product around the Kansas City metro area, and a comfortable turf that I could call my own. This was an area between The Country Club Plaza and downtown that was convenient for navigating and meeting people from all walks of life. I felt more like a salesman managing a territory than a person breaking the law on a daily basis. I went about my business in a lively manner without a care to the dangers looming around every corner.

I had even forged a friendship with my neighbor who was solid enough to let me use her driveway regularly, as long as my vehicle wasn't parked behind hers when she had to leave for work first thing in the morning.

Stationed behind her car in the driveway, I sat doing the usual safety checks around my periphery while gathering my phone, bag, and other belongings. This had come to be a necessary practice after years of working in a black-market business. Basically, I had to make sure I wasn't followed or about to get robbed.

Prepared now to leave my vehicle and venture inside, I opened the driver's side door and noticed a saucy moistness in the air. It was that fresh time of year, a moment of release from the chill of winter. When I was younger, I cherished early evenings like this, knowing that baseball and country cruising were on the horizon. But that wasn't what was on my mind these days. I wasn't considering the joy of the changing of seasons or gawking at girls outside the local Dairy Queen. With thousands of dollars in cash and often tens of thousands in drugs on me at any point in time, I was preoccupied and anxious. At this stage in my life, I was only concerned with moving product and funneling money to the right people. These concerns fueled my evenings of toil and torment. That night was a typical run through the Plaza route with some clowning around in between. "Sure," I thought, "I'll just block my neighbor's car for a few minutes while I run inside my house to gather a few things." Being a responsible salaried employee and law-abiding citizen, she was most likely asleep anyway.

Soon I'd dash off again and be on to my next deal anyhow.

I rushed to the entrance of my house, slid in, and pulled the door shut behind me, locking it immediately of course. The house I lived in flaunted 20-foot ceilings that peaked in the center while having a series of ledges and overhangs that held large wine bottles and European-themed statues as decorations. This home had a cheesy remodel done in the 1980s and was often referred to by my friends as the Kung-Fu Porn studio because of the bamboo trim and large well-equipped bathroom just inside the back deck. The shower was large enough for several people, which I had experienced several times. A vacant spot where the once thriving hot tub lived was now occupied by a glass table that was prime for pushing around drugs. A large bamboo-framed mirror hung proudly over the extended sink area on the south wall, sentry and steady in the room. Certainly a poor man's Boogie Nights since it lacked a pool and three-car garage.

Life didn't seem strange to me at the time and so neither would the character of this place where I lived. There was a stairwell built in the center of the home that led up to a loft that I used as a bedroom and storage for my products. This loft peered out over the rest of my house and had a window directly over the front door that faced out into the front yard. It was a good observation point since it had an overlooking view of both the inside and outside of my house. I also had video equipment installed with monitors in the loft where I could watch the events around my property through eight cameras I had hidden. This was my command center and main base of operations.

After I entered my house and breezed upstairs, I rummaged through my stash of assorted pills needed for the next deal

I'd set up. I counted out OxyContin, Adderall, Xanax, and Ecstasy, which were among the things that the most recent caller would probably be interested in. We didn't discuss details over the phone, only if a meeting in the near future would be possible. I already had balls of white powder separated in little zip bags ready to unload, and I was aware that this customer was enamored with the varieties of pills that I could provide. I quickly counted the money I had with me and decided to hide most of it while keeping a few hundred on me to spend.

While I focused on the next several hours' errands, I began to formulate a plan, a route, and to allow time for any other precautions that may be necessary. Like any other business, one learns from experience, and in the drug trade one usually does not get second chances. Lessons learned were often harsh and damaging, if not dangerous and altogether lethal. I was a bit hurried that evening, but at some point, I always was. It was nothing to be alarmed over, or so I thought.

Stuffing pills into various packages, I sat at my desk for a few minutes peeking at my monitors. My right knee was bouncing up and down with a nervous jaunt. The back deck was dark and quiet that evening. Every so often a raccoon would set off the sensors and the whole backyard would become bright as day. The greenhouse on the east side was quiet too. It would be nice to have some of my people over to spruce things up in there. I loved taking care of plants and was somewhat ashamed that I didn't take the time to tend to them myself. Paying someone for every chore in my life had become the new normal. My job was to keep the drug users of KC fed while everything else took a backseat.

Then, like the subtle shock of watching those first films of the atomic bombs explode from a distance, I saw the main camera watching my front walkway burst with illumination. I wondered with gleeful awe if it was authentic and began to realize that my little urban compound was being invaded. Shocked, but not surprised, I watched a black van screech to a stop as armed men filed out to my front door. They were orderly, well-equipped, and certainly moved with a purpose. It was quite a rush just seeing it unfold, but that feeling quickly dissipated into anxiety and fear. The words that screamed over and over through my head were, "Well, here we go! Here we go!" and frustration began to taint my already toxic demeanor. This was the moment that I had tried to suppress but knew was an eventuality. I wasn't foolish enough to believe that I could live in the drug trade forever. There was no time to do anything substantial, although being on my second-floor loft allowed several extra key seconds to prepare myself to be handled. I could tell they were the authorities because they moved in a systematic fashion. I was frozen for a few seconds as I watched them on my monitors. It was like some strange interactive reality show where I was the target. Now that would be a fucked-up game, huh? To heck with these escape rooms that everyone loves these days. Can you imagine being in some sort of simulated activity where you paid to witness what it's like to be involved in a home invasion?

I remember thinking I wish I were more prepared and organized for their arrival. I had illicit items stretched all over the loft and no time to dispose of any of them. Inching over to the window that overlooked my front yard, I saw what I assumed was the SWAT team solidify and burst through my front door. None of them remained stationed in the front yard. So, without thinking, I opened the window and jumped out with no plan, only chemical-fueled ambition to prolong this dangerous fantasy life I'd been thriving in for far too long.

My whole life up through my teens was somewhat privileged, my father a surgeon and my mother running the daily routines. It was a quintessential rural, white, all-American upbringing. There were little league games and ice cream socials at church in the summertime. Festivals and school plays reminded me of my winters. A loving family and active neighborhood were common throughout our town and it was hard to go anywhere without running into someone who knew you by name. Comfortable if not quaint.

We took family vacations throughout the United States. There were numerous jaunts to Europe, Canada, and Mexico. I especially liked learning Spanish with my father on our trips south of the border. He would make us kids speak to the waiter in Spanish at any restaurant we went to. It helped us understand social awareness at a young age. Our trips to Canada were mostly camping adventures that in my adolescent mind rivaled any Lewis and Clark expedition. My parents instilled in us the appreciation of nature, culture, and the state of all humankind. I probably didn't thank them enough growing up.

High school was the same. I dated pretty girls and we would cruise around our small town in my 1969 Barracuda. My pals and I would swill beers on country roads and take midnight swims in our friend's pool. I excelled at baseball, football, and basketball enough to letter and consider pursuing sports in college. My parents taught the importance of good morals and yet were lenient enough to let us be kids and enjoy ourselves. John Mellencamp would have been proud.

I left this small community for the nearby University of Kansas in Lawrence. Attending there wasn't with aspirations to start a drug empire or make money illegally. I worked for the college newspaper, the **University Daily Kansan,** *where I stored up knowledge about journalism, advertising, and sales. I got As and Bs while learning how to work hard and play hard at the same time. I knew graduating from college would bring on responsibility, and I was excited to start making real-world money. In the meantime, I made sure I enjoyed myself as much as possible while continuing to educate, enlighten, and encourage others around me with as much positivity as I could muster. Every day was happy, healthy, and free. An American dream, if I do say so myself. It's such a shame how this charming life did not foreshadow the reality I would live years later.*

Repetitive wrong choices and continual lies are what got me from there to here—lies to myself, the only person that it should be impossible to lie to. It's a metamorphosis that occurred very carefully, methodically and over the course of some wild years. This is the contrast that is simply crazy to me now.

Staring back into history I saw my life's timeline that went from so pampered and good to so shocking and unraveled. Supplementing this strange separation, there were no disasters or daunting events that swayed my behavior. I wasn't treated badly as a kid. There was no abuse or learning disabilities to deal with. No major life changes that would make growing into a man difficult. Only, I did have a feeling of always trying to live up to my successful father's expectations. Today though, bad judgement on my part got way out of control and led to throwing myself out of a window to avoid a SWAT invasion.

Life has a funny way of flushing things out into the open to be dealt with one way or another. A person never really believes that a ride in the fast lane will end, especially suddenly and certainly like this. If you're clever enough to get away with living by the hustle for years, then it becomes part of you and mainstream life seems like it's for suckers or people who don't think big enough. Maybe this was some sort of compensation or shortcut to success so I could impress my pops.

Well, God has a way of taking out the trash and shaking things up enough to humble a person to his core to remind him of whose plan is really in play in this universe. Hint: It's not us humans. I now accept that this April evening was not like the others. My biggest concern wasn't if I was going to be ripped off or noticed by some of the people in the real world. No, those were small beans compared to the federal authorities, and I realized now that my suppressed fears were true. I was being watched, set up, and the years of counting stacks of money in my living room were a thing of folklore now.

I was frantic as I jumped out of my second story window and landed in my front yard. I considered my options but quickly decided to dart out into the road and up to the intersection of Corbin Terrace (yes, I lived on a street bearing my first name) and Summit Street. This quiet neighborhood a few blocks north of the Country Club Plaza was now ground zero in my life's biggest turning point to date. I ran with fury, not for a second thinking I would get away from this situation unharmed. It wasn't hard to notice there were several government vehicles angled in at the corner and numerous official looking people milling about waiting for the Special Weapons and Tactics team to pull me out of my house. Here is the only part of this memory that still makes me giggle a little bit when I recall these events. In all my blazing glory, I ran toward them and saw the astonished looks on their faces as they watched me wiggle past and jet south toward the Plaza. I temporarily got away and would later be informed by KCMO PD that they were very pissed off because of my escape. I know I sounded like a crazy man saying out loud as I ran past them, "...WHAT THE!" It didn't make any sense to me either, only that those are the thoughts that were running through my head. It's not too clever to mock one's pursuers, especially when they are part of the largest tactical force in the nation.

Running away from my house and the shadows of authority figures, my mind was frenzied and free. My thoughts drifted to a time years before when I would play backyard football with my buddies. Crispy autumn air always had me smiling, and the scratch of stray crunchy leaves under my feet was the only setting for a pick-up game—shifting away from would-be tacklers and running toward open space in my neighbor's yard, the end zone in sight again.

This present moment brought on the same emotions. Football was fun and rowdy, but I hated getting tackled, so I learned to run like the wind. My dad always reminded me that, "... if I weren't the biggest guy on the field, then I had better be one of the fastest." Those words stuck with me throughout all my high school sports. Speed was my biggest asset. My pops with the sound advice and my mother with the ever-loving encouragement. They were both supportive in all my endeavors.

But tonight was different. I had nobody to cheer me on, only the fanfare in my head and fear in my heart. The words, "What the ..." that came out of my mouth were not for me. It was my mocking impression of the cops waiting for me at the end of the block. In my attempted escape from this harrowing situation, I hurried past my abductors. Looking them in the eyes, I was saying out loud what they surely must be thinking at this very moment. I had smoked meth that night, probably did some coke too. I had burned some pot to calm me down and, at some point, even taken some Xanax, just for fun of course. My brain was confounded and the adrenaline coursing through my nervous system spiked as my eyes were splayed wide open.

The memories as a speedster from my younger days were jumbled with sarcastic parody as I passed the authorities at the end of my street. My actions that night have stamped out that incident in the history of Corbin Terrace forever. This small, quiet neighborhood just north of the Plaza wasn't ready for such an event, yet there I loped through the streets like a madman, operating on childhood memories and drug induced ambition. Certainly not a combination that I had considered before nor practiced ever since.

It was like a movie scene—ducking through yards, going in and out of buildings, and using all the verve a human body can muster. The streets and surroundings were stretches of light across my sight, and my legs resembled Charlie Chaplin scurrying down a stairway in an old black and white film. I knew it was all over and I somewhat expected to be shot in the back or tripped from behind, but I continued on while a muddled plan came to mind. My girlfriend lived only a few blocks from me, so I headed toward the Bradwood Condominiums on Jefferson. This was just up the hill from Tomfooleries on 47th Street and only two blocks to the south of my house. I made my way through her pool area and began a hurried banging on her door. Boy, this was going to stir up a commotion among her neighbors. They were good, quiet people and in no way could have been prepared for the upheaval about to occur.

Additionally, my girlfriend didn't approve of my nefarious activities. Day after day she would try to get me to spend time with her doing "couple stuff." She supportively counseled me to cease the shady dealings and pursue one of the many other

12

careers I was qualified to do. She was a gem and was about to be one of the many things that would soon crumble around me in the years to come. This night, though, I arrived at her place with crazy eyes and a slew of agents in tow. The priority now was to see her just so I could hug her one last time before breaking her heart. There was no getting away from this heat.

She answered the door and looked at me as if I were Sasquatch —bewildered, scared, and sad because she realized what was going on and knew that trouble in the form of the authorities had caught up to me in a big way. Immediately crying, she let me in and we fled to the bedroom where I hugged her tightly and then laid down on her waterbed to catch my breath ... I could hardly breathe, see, or feel anymore. There was banging and yelling from the other side of the wall, and then a heavy smash as they busted the door in off its hinges. I heard the pounding of feet heading into the back room to arrest me.

I was flailing about trying to fight being apprehended when I was thrown on the floor and felt the pain of a man standing on my neck holding a pistol to my temple. They thought I had a weapon, so they were using precaution, but I began to black out. The events over the next 15 minutes are somewhat hazy. An ambulance was called, I was carried outside, and Emma (not her real name) cried hysterically. She looked so beautiful that night in her above the knee nighty wrapped tightly around her freshly showered body. Most anything else in her condo that night is a blur except the memory of her kneeling on the floor sobbing and pleading with the men taking me away.

The images of my life flashed through my head like you imagine they do when you die. I even questioned if my body had perished and began thinking about all the things I would regret or what I would be missing out on. Why wasn't I spending time with her tonight? Who convinced me to chase a career in which no one can ever truly succeed? How come I hadn't seen or spoken with my family in months? Life might have been beautiful if I had made some different choices, but now everything was dark and confusing.

During the blackout, my mind drifted to peaceful places, like some sort of protection from the shock. I had long desired to cease my operations. Moving the drugs, doing the drugs and being around the people were devastating to my soul. I felt stuck in the world I had created and all the while sinking deeper into the swamp. There was a monster in my life. Greed and the guilt brought on by the pursuit of it. My shortcuts never brought me within reach of the success I sought, and shame would soon replace the politeness of my guilt.

Emma was still on my unconscious mind, recalling all of her recent efforts to help me stop my drug use. The blackout evoked memories from just 30 days prior of her constructing a little leather binder to carry in my pocket. It had pretty little paisleys stenciled on the cover and thick grey pages bound together with days of the week printed on each one. In this pocketbook I was to keep track of the times of each day that I would use drugs and the amounts. This was an effort to curb my consumption. If it was apparent to me how much and when I was using drugs, then maybe I would work toward getting away from the sickening activities.

I cried when she first handed it to me. We were alone in her condo and she had serious, sorrowful eyes. Her explanation began simply. "Let's try something. I made this for you to help us get better. You are a different person than you're supposed to be. This might help you get off drugs." She cared, wanted to help, and labored to do so. Something I wouldn't even do for myself.

This little pocketbook helped temporarily. After two weeks of keeping track of my drug usage, my consumption had decreased dramatically. Staring myself in the face every time I thought about using and actually taking the time to keep track of it was genius on her part. I could see myself moving in the right direction and gave her all the credit for my progress. In about two weeks' time I went from smoking about five grams of crack a day to about one gram. This was still a significant amount, but not debilitating.

My problem involved more than me, though. People were contacting me every day about drugs, and I couldn't stay away from the money. I had positioned myself in too many different facets of the distribution chain. Besides moving large amounts of cocaine, I would also do side deals and obtain pills and pot to personalize my deals for each customer. Whether it was keeping my distributors stocked up or procuring Xanax to trade for more coke, I was a jester juggling too much stress for a healthy life.

For the two weeks of progress from the "pocketbook plan" I congratulated myself with 96 hours of wide-awake indulging. Things were now right back to where they were before, and probably worse.

I had numerous bouts with recovery and sobriety, but it was Emma's pocketbook challenge that swam through my mind now. Just one last reminder of her attempts to love me and now, how much I would miss her for the years to come. This knocked-out dream was the closest I had come to a clear mind in years, and I relished every deep-seated moment.

It was Lou Reed's "Perfect Day" that began to serenade me as my consciousness was sucked back into the world of the living.

I woke up in the hospital to members of the SWAT team hovering just outside my room. Yes, they looked pissed. Yes,

I was alive, but the outlook was certainly bleak for starters. It was somewhat comforting to be on a hospital cot knowing that this was probably the most comfortable bed I would be on for a while. I was certain they had enough to lock me up for a few years at least. I was caught red-handed with product and money. Things did not look good, but I thought I would always get a second chance. Right? I mean, I was no Larry Hoover, just a guy who got in a little too deep. I would just calmly apologize for my misdoings and gladly cease my dealings of hard, illicit, illegal substances. There, problem solved.

Suddenly the SWAT commander entered the room with the rest of his crew close behind. Things got a lot more serious, and he began to go over the situation with me. "Are you Mr. Corbin Bosl..vaco..lac? Do you reside at 724 Corbin Terrace?"

Curtly, I replied, "Yes ... and yes."

"Where were you running off to this evening?" I could sense some sarcasm, but it wasn't to his benefit.

A target is not supposed to get away. That's the one reason they showed up to my house that night, to apprehend me and take me into custody. They finally got me after a nice little chase, but their superior, as I was told later by a KCPD officer, reprimanded them in front of all their peers. I'll assume that this does not go over well in a fraternity of guys such as this. He explained that I was under arrest for the distribution of narcotics and that they were serving a no-knock warrant. This meant that a judge approved the authorities to legally enter my residence by force and without warning. He was presented enough evidence to brand me a nuisance to society.

The SWAT commander continued, "We entered the domicile looking for marijuana and cocaine. How long have you been distributing cocaine? Do you manufacture amphetamines?

Who else is involved?" I was in no mood for conversation, so I acknowledged that I wasn't talking to him. He had me sign the warrant and explained I was in custody and would be transferred to a nearby correctional institution as soon as I was released by the hospital. Yes, this would definitely be the most comfortable bed I would have for a while.

Then the healthcare staff entered the room with a flurry of different questions all pertaining to my health and well-being. The nurses all said I looked like hell run over and wanted a list of all the different drugs I was on. Alcohol was not on the list, but anything that could be burned or snorted was. The attendants were actually friendly and took care of me as if I had genuine needs and a future ahead of me. Didn't they understand it was over with? All of it. The game was up. The only relief was that I wasn't running anymore. Not tonight from the cops. Not tomorrow from reality. Not in life toward the monster.

As I breathed fresh oxygen from the mask they had given me, I began to calm down in the moment but felt ambiguity when envisioning my future. How would I adjust to being in institutions? It would be prison, the crazy house, or wherever they decided I would properly reside. Was this what was best for me? Sure it was. It was a relief, and I now had an unmistakable excuse to pull out of the life I had been living in recent years, a life that was breaking me down. An existence that was opposed to my upbringing and beliefs. Somehow, I knew that the decisions I made going forward would define me for the rest of my life. This incident was the shock I needed to start taking one right step after another. This arrest was not going to be the end of me.

Hours later, I was transferred from St. Luke's Hospital in Westport to the Kansas City, Missouri city jail. The drive there was sad for me. I couldn't really see outside of the vehicle, but I imagined what part of the city we were moving through, wondering when I would see these streets again. My head swarmed with silent goodbyes to people I may not see for a while like my friends Autumn and Cristian, my brother Tyler, and my mother. "Oh mom, I'm so terribly sorry. This is not how life is supposed to go."

I even offered farewells to McCoy's and Harry's, two establishments in Westport that were on my mind that evening. I was suddenly plucked out of the world, my whereabouts out of my control. When would I be on the streets again? This was a symbolic funeral procession and I was entombed in this metal casket rolling through the roadways of my favorite city.

Intake into the jail downtown was even worse. This was the start of living behind locked doors and concrete walls, oppression, and depression. After giving up my wallet, belt, shoelaces, and watch, I was plunked down inside a holding cell with a few benches and toilets. Everyone in there was pissed and looking to take out their frustrations on someone. I assumed it would probably be the newest guy just because I was the person with freedom most recently in his rearview. I kept quiet and crouched on the floor near an open corner, hoping it wasn't already spoken for. There were only a few things I understood about jail at this point in my life. Real estate was at a premium, and Darwin's maxim "survival of the fittest" was law above all others.

Crouched down in a grubby corner, I attempted to appear sturdy and in control. I paid close attention to my surroundings without looking up, face forward, but not at any person in particular. My hands clenched my shoulders from the chill while my mouth smacked with the taste of muddy paint. Not an ounce of hope stemmed from any soul in this holding cell. Speaking didn't cross my mind, and thinking was like trying to fit a baseball in my ear. The bleak surroundings made my chest grow heavier with every breath, and it was all I could do not to freak out.

But I could not freak out, no way. I closed my eyes and with extreme effort I gathered my wits to assess my situation. Something stuck with me sharply that night. It was strange why this was my biggest concern at this particular time. After all that had occurred, the foot chase, Emma crying, being hospitalized, and knowing that my house would be ransacked, I recalled that my Mercedes was still parked behind my neighbor's car in her driveway. How pissed was she going to be when she tried to go to work the next morning and saw my car blocking her in.

One of the few photos taken inside the Corbin Terrace house in 2009.

Sports shaped much of my life through high school.

PERSPIRATION YEARS

"You couldn't relive your life, skipping the awful parts,
without losing what made it worthwhile."
—*The Odds: A Love Story*, Stewart O'Nan

*There was a guy, we'll call him Z, and he was loyal as all get
out. My goal in dealing drugs was to create as many loyal dealers
underneath me as possible. He was the most dependable.*

*After reading several books, I used Robert Kiyosaki's methods
of surrounding myself with competent people and creating a distribution network. This way I could multiply my efforts through
all the people I had underneath me, with the money eventually
being funneled up to me. I took care of them all the best I could,
and I told myself that I was a good employer, providing for these
people.*

*On days when I had been high for too long, Z would run errands
for me. Collecting money, dropping off more product, and going
to the hardware store for supplies. He fixed cars, gave advice,
and kept people away from me when I was on edge. Ours was
a precarious business, but we treated it like it was real, and our
efforts paid off while we were open.*

I didn't know it at the time, but Z later told me the reason why he was so loyal during those years of running errands around Kansas City.

One evening there were several people at my downtown loft. We were all squaring things away to get out and about for the evening. I was busy weighing drugs to pass around to my distributors so they could make some money while out on the town.

At this point, I had known Z for a few months through another friend of mine. He was there hanging around as I was trying to get cleaned up and ready for the evening. A downstairs neighbor kept bugging me for 40 buck's worth of coke, but I was ignoring him. Didn't want to deal with it. It was too small to worry about and too risky to do exchanges like that with people near my own place.

But I was greedy, and I thought about using this opportunity to show off a little. I got the brilliant idea to give Z the bag of coke and asked him to go downstairs and trade it for the 40 bucks. I had a plan to see if he was someone who wanted to get involved in the business I was building. It was a small enough deal to monitor as a sort of tryout for the job. He obliged without question and returned only minutes later with my money. Immediately I put 20 dollars in my pocket and gave him the other 20. He had done me the favor and I wanted to show him that I would pay for good help and loyal soldiers. It was a small show of gratitude, but good enough to make a point. I was able to illustrate how I wanted to start building my business network, and I figured this was a good opportunity to give everyone around that night a visual example of what that meant.

Well, this effort made an impression on him. At the time, Z wasn't working a regular job and was hard up for cash. That happened to be the first money he had made in weeks. He expressed to me that if I took care of him, then he would do the same for me, and so began a working relationship that lasted several years. Our system worked for a while and was a well-run machine. It has been amusing for me to ponder how small gestures can lead to larger undertakings.

This probably isn't the way most people want to remember their past. It isn't glamorous to build people up through black market business practices. It's illegal and dangerous. But it is part of my history, and I remember the human side of our dealings. I was truly trying to manage people well and help them make money—help us all make money. It was just the wrong vehicle to do so. Today I strive to do the same things in helping people grow, only through more positive and respectable means.

After the bust, it took a few years to dwindle my life down to a point where I finally self-surrendered and pled guilty to 90 months in federal prison. In the meantime, I was let out of jail on pretrial bond. I had several months to get my affairs in order before I started my stint.

The Feds charged me with Conspiracy to Distribute Cocaine. During this period, I was broke and hardly able to pay for anything to keep up a normal life. Rent was always late and short while meals were on the cheap side. I often paid for gas with a handful of change and didn't really drive too far from my own neighborhood.

A part-time job at the Westport-area hardware store kept me afloat. Reporting to a pretrial officer and counselor several times a month gave me a taste of what my life was about to become—institutional in nature and strict with rules and guidelines. Everything was slowing down to my eventual incarceration that was looming over my head. It was depressing, but I did my best to take in every free moment before my dreadful day of the lockup.

Focusing my mind on simpler things while getting ready for all of the unknowns that were about to overtake my being started to consolidate my view of the world. Everything had to do with preparing myself to get through this next chunk of my life.

It was a struggle as I used drugs, drank, and cried in fits and bursts. I wasn't supposed to use drugs on pretrial release, and I was tested regularly to make sure of that. The protocol was strict; I had to call in every day to see what my status was. Living was extremely sad as I would sit alone, pity myself, worry about the authorities, and then find ways to circumvent my urine tests to keep up the charade. A horrible existence, if not a 24/7 anxiety attack.

I lost pace quickly, and after failing several drug tests I was warned that I had zero chances left. If I failed again, I would be sent to federal holding immediately.

This was the tipping point.

Somehow, out of pure fear and shame I just quit. I took a deep breath and plugged my way through. There is no glamorous way of explaining the process.

Every day I would spend numerous hours alone before going to work. There was worrying, concentrating, and self-grieving, willing myself to be a better person and stay away from the junk. I focused on the present, the only thing that really mattered. My existence was literally minute-to-minute.

At work I just concentrated on the tasks at hand. I was diligent in finding ways to occupy my mind. There was always work to do at a hardware store, and I was grateful for the bustle of the place.

I was a wreck, but my eyes were wide open, and I was scared of going to prison. If it were eventually going to happen, I just decided in my heart, one moment after another, that I would do it like a man. I had been playing games like a kid for years, and if this wasn't going to be my moment of truth, then I was doomed. There were moments of peace in my heart that I didn't understand until years later. God was tickling my neck, but I didn't turn fully to Him until I was behind bars and alone.

I somehow found a way to make my life meaningful again. It was a simplification process as I sorted out daily duties and activities to find joy in each thing I did. There wasn't a way to explain it as I was going through the daily procedures, but looking back on it now, I know how to put it into words. It was action and attempt while at the center of it all was a spiritual force that was guiding me through, whether I wanted to accept it or not.

There were certain days I would focus on the natural world. On a walk to work, I would take the long route and enjoy gardens as I plodded past. Bursting flowers and spry budding trees boasted the youth of spring. Manicured landscape became a pleasure to me again. In the years previous, I wouldn't even know what season it was, let alone appreciate the perpetual rolling time of nature. A whiff of fresh cut grass or new cedar mulch gave me a sense of calm and appreciation of the present, whatever the day was offering.

Other days, I would concentrate on mending relationships with those close to me whom I had ignored for years. Mostly family and a few stray friends would be on the top of my mind, and I became thoughtful in my interactions with them again. This might have been due to the fear I had of being separated from everyone once I would be incarcerated, but nonetheless fear can be a motivator. Why not let it be for good instead of evil?

Most people that I had been making money with selling illegal drugs were not talking to me anymore, so it was easy to simplify my interactions with others. It was a lonely existence, but deep down I felt this was my chance to make good before I was too far gone. If nothing else, it was a ripe opportunity to get something meaningful out of this life.

With that attitude I started to realize that it is never too late. If my intentions were pure then people recognized that. Especially after being sober for several months, I really started to notice the respect coming back into my life. Family members were requesting favors of me and I really felt like there was usefulness again.

It was small things really. My grandmother asking me to help her move some furniture, or a neighbor down the street asking if I wanted to join her for coffee on the porch. Normal, helpful, enlightening activities that I now recognized value in. Before, I only evaluated merit in things with a "what's in it for me" attitude. Greedy and selfish. Somehow now, humility had found me, and I was relishing the new feelings of peace and serenity in my life.

All these things began to happen because of my attitude with the world around me. I didn't follow some 12-step process or attend some expensive counseling sessions. My days were chopped up into 15-minute segments and I would proceed through each day living presently in those segments. My health became more important as I was now treating my body with more esteem and interest. I read books again, something that I loved to do once in my life but had lost along the way.

Conversations with people were now about the energy of the words and not the time of day or schedule I was on. I took interest in others more keenly, mainly to take the attention off myself and my blunders. I found, though, that attentiveness toward others brought joy back into my life. The world is a large, wonderful place, and my story is not the only one to be told or heard. By listening to the day-to-day strife and mundaneness as others reflected on their lives, I realized that I, too, could appreciate these small things.

Life didn't have to be about the rise to power or attainment of dollars. It could be about putzing around the yard with a cup of coffee in the morning, evaluating the progress of tomato plants on the verge of fruit. The jewels of time that I had dismissed for my chase of the fast life were still there to value if I only relearned the way to see again.

So it happened that way, in boring little tidbits. During my 15-minute segments throughout the days before I went to prison, I learned again how to appreciate the simplicity of life. It may have been fear that was the underlying motivator but, regardless, I trudged through the final six months or so of my pretrial clean from drugs. The thought of doing them even sickened me a little bit. I accepted that my run was over. My personal health was to become my new focus as I had a deep-seated yearning to make up for the years I had wasted being wasted.

At my Aunt's wedding in 1986. From left to right Corbin, father Dr. Joe, little sister Kristin, mother Cheryl, and brother Tyler.

In 2008 the drug use and lifestyle started to get a little haywire.

WHEN IT SETS IN

"No man knows how bad he is
till he has tried very hard to be good."
—C.S. Lewis

*Lord God, today we thank You for living in the land of the free
and the home of the brave. We know that we have it better than
so many other people, no matter our current situation. Help
us today to remember that our true liberty lies in our personal
decision to protect our heart, mind, and body from evil influences.
We pray now for true freedom in our lives, Lord. Freedom from
sin. Right now, in the name of Jesus we repent to You, God.
Forgive us of our sins, our wrongdoings, those things that were
not pleasing to You. Release us from our anxieties, all useless
worry in the hope of coming closer to You, Lord God, so we may
live within your will for us. Help us to realize, Lord, that your will
for us is all truth, pure love perfect in the kingdom of Heaven.*

###

So, fast-forward a few years into my sentence and understand
that I had taken my own self-help to a level of encouragement.

The activities I was doing to spend my time in prison were actually helping my mental state. I would often write in prison as a release from my angst and to keep my mind from being distracted by the broad picture that our existence is.

My time with the Feds was eating me up by this point and looking back, it was my spiritual life that was my strength. I read the entreaty that preceded this chapter to a group of men who had gathered at a support group on the evening of July 4, 2016. After writing this prayer in my journal and then reading it out loud to our group, there were several petitions, prayers if you will, from other men that were specific to what was going on in the institution I was housed in that particular summer. Some guy was having family problems, a friend of mine was in the SHU, and I was praying for a judge to commute my sentence per some motions made to the court. Anything to get some relief from this place and get back to reality.

Journaling and sharing my writings in prison became a saving grace to myself and the men who joined me in our various prayer groups. None of us were trying to become preachers or Bible beaters; we were only sharing our grievances and using our higher power to help guide us during these trying years. It was a belief in the energy of the universe that we shared, and the details of those beliefs didn't matter. Only that we could share our experiences together and not suffer alone.

The essence of my divine beliefs began to improve three years earlier while I was housed in a federal holding facility at St. Claire County Jail in Osceola, Missouri. It was in this place that my tour through the federal system started and took its mighty grip on my being. The enormity of everything—my relationships, my safety, my core beliefs, my sobriety, my sanity—it was all tested from the very start.

How simple a day can be when everything tangible is stripped away and the bare essentials are all that are left with which to conduct your whole life. Most everything else is shared. Bathrooms, eating, and seeing your counselor are all just part of the large machine that warehouses you and thousands of other men who are looking for a glimmer of meaning in their now meager existence.

So I first started to hate it, all of it. I bucked the system that was holding me hostage, I ignored the other people who were now my entire community, and I tried to convince myself that I could just white knuckle it until I finally got out of this mess. If you want to go crazy, then try these methods, but sooner or later you have to let the wave of your situation wash over you and accept where you are and what you are experiencing. I had to become my situation. Once this takes place, the days may still be crappy, but they are your crappy. There's significance in this because finally making something yours gives you some of your strength back. You own it, and that is the start to rebuilding your own foundation.

It was there in that cramped holding facility where I broke down and realized my sentence was going to be a marathon and not a sprint. Like it or not, this was my reality now. It was a struggle accepting my situation, and I was certainly fair game for veteran inmates to prey on me and my obvious weaknesses. Being new to prison life, I was naïve and somewhat scared of people or events that I didn't understand, or care to understand for that matter. I was also not a big, tough, strong guy, so my physical attributes weren't intimidating either. But here I was, thrust into this situation, so I started to think about what strengths I had to draw upon that would help me get along in this new life of mine. I knew that I was smart with organizing

34

and leading people, so I looked around to see how I could be an asset to the shot-callers in cell block H.

The funny thing is that almost immediately I began noticing God speaking to me in ways I had never experienced before.

Before going to prison, I was far from spiritual. I still had interests in the mysteries of life, its meanings, and our purposes here, but it wasn't God centered or anything like my Catholic upbringing from my childhood. But being locked in a small room, all day in my case, led to what felt like a continual anxiety attack. Being short of breath and weary of what my future would hold was a drain emotionally. I knew that my life was reshaping itself and I would emerge from this experience, however long it would last, a new human. The question remained though, would this new person be better and stronger or simply damaged goods, like I felt at that moment.

After being locked in there for about a week, I longed to stretch my legs, to at least just walk around the corner or down the hall. How sweet it would be to get a glimpse of the outside. Cinder blocks and orange jumpsuits were my only scenery, and I missed the smell of autumn leaves falling on the Westport neighborhoods where I spent so many years before. Being new to jail, it was difficult to get my old neighborhood out of my head. I remember asking my cellmate if the guards would let me go outside for five minutes so long as I asked nicely. He got a huge laugh out of that and thanked me for the amusement. I missed my front porch, and it occurred to me that I might not ever see it again.

I was fantasizing about a brisk wind blowing against my face while walking down Jefferson Street, when all of the sudden one of the correctional officers opened our cell block door and asked if anyone wanted to go to a prayer group. My ears perked up at the opportunity to do anything or go anywhere else other than where I was. I must have looked like Cosmo Kramer from Seinfeld, eager to do whatever Jerry was asking him to do. Nobody else was really interested in the idea to attend anything "churchy," so I was definitely now set out differently in front of everyone. It was a little unnerving, but I decided I didn't care.

I got up off the bunk and stepped outside of my cell not knowing what to expect. There were three of us that assembled just inside the exit door of the pod, and we stood in line with our heads faced forward and hands clasped behind our backs. This was as exciting as I could have imagined, and my heart fluttered with the pitter-patter of adolescent love. I was leaving my crowded, stinky, cold cell and getting a reprieve. I didn't care if they wanted us to scrub the guard's bathroom with a toothbrush; I was actually getting to leave the cell block.

I felt unqualified to attend a prayer group, what with my ignoring God for so many years. But this tug that I felt in my chest was interesting. It was light and hopeful. Different than anything that money or drugs had given me in the years leading up to this moment.

We were marched down the hall and into a tight room that only fit about six chairs snugly. I was a little disappointed that I was now in an even smaller room that contradicted my plan for a temporary respite from my previous situation of jibber-jabber and despair. Quickly, a calm came over me as a woman entered the room with a friendly smile and frumpy demeanor. She talked about the weather getting cooler outside, inquired if we were being treated fairly, and asked if we, too, were treating our captors with respect. It was so nice to have a touch of reality within reach again. She smelled of the outdoors, and I was again reminded of the changing of the seasons. In my short stint in Osceola, MO, I already longed for real shoes, underwear that fit, some kind of comb or brush for my hair, and soap that didn't smell and feel like sheetrock. The feeling of deprivation from everything in the real world is the first of many unsettling events that unfold in a jail or prison setting.

So, the lady—I cannot for the life of me even remember her name—sat down and asked a straightforward question that hit me like a ton of bricks. She asked if any or all of us had accepted Jesus Christ as our Lord and Savior and if we believed in the teachings of the Bible. I had gone to Catholic school as a kid and grew up oblivious to the idea that there were people who did not have Jesus in their lives. But I was also oblivious to the idea of what that even meant in the first place. Like so many children growing up, I had just gone through the motions when it came to church stuff. So, my answer to her question was a blumbering "Sure!" I simply wanted to get this group started in the right direction and share the glimmer of hope that was blooming in my heart.

Then she took a step back, opened the Bible, and explained what she meant and how important it was to accept Jesus into your life. For the next hour, I enjoyed her words with the wonderment of a child witnessing the circus for the first time. Talking about how fulfilling it is to pray about our cares and worries and letting Jesus take away our burdens and fears. These things that seemed so simple yet so helpful, especially for someone struggling as much as myself, were now a seed of optimism to my life's weary foundation. We discussed how to pray, how to settle our minds in a combative world, and what to continue to do after she left that night. The joy I felt from our time spent together was far better than what I expected it to be. I had simply wanted a short break from our cramped quarters.

By visiting the jail that evening, this courageous woman was doing God's work. She was planting seeds of inspiration that He could now germinate and nurture in each of our individual souls. I was pushed to writing that night to reflect on paper what I was feeling in my heart so this moment could be remembered. It dawned on me that maybe writing would help with my anxiety, despair, and boredom. Here is what was written in my journal upon my return to H pod in the front section of that small federal holding facility in Osceola, Missouri. I would have never constructed these words together in the previous years of my life, but here they just flowed out like tightly wound tension in a wonderful spindle of relief:

The most important thing in life, the meaning of life is to be aligned with God's energy ... the light of the universe. One of the ways we as humans do this is through prayer. God, give me the foresight to continue in prayer with you as much as possible. By doing this I feel closer to You as I bring my soul into Your greatness. Help me through life as I cast my wants, worries, and troubles to You while giving You all the praise I can offer up for the goodness and love You bring to my life. Give me the strength to value my prayer time with You and not be distracted by worldly sins. Let me bask in Your presence and be guided by the Holy Spirit. Amen.

Writing this simple prayer was not earth-shattering in itself, but the release and ray of hope it brought me in these initial murky times was what I needed. It helped to propel my path into a meaningful direction where I was able to start rebuilding my foundation. What became apparent was that prayer and meditation are keenly relevant to attaining a beautiful life. This practice of consistent prayer was just what I needed to move on to the next thing. I suppose this was the first event of real purpose that I recall from my initial days in jail.

Now, a second event occurred upon my return to the unit that evening. I was thrust back into the heavy-headed stress of what defines most federal holding facilities. Tension in these places is amped up all the time, and dealing with it is a battle from lights on to lights out. It was around 8 p.m. when we returned and the energy in the unit was red-lining out of control. A combination of people talking and moving around, with others harassing each other, watching TV, yelling at the TV, and lurking about in their cells. Finally, it was the three of us who had just returned who were quickly being drained of our heightened sense of awareness most recently gained from our prayer group during the past hour. A feeling of nausea came over me, and like a glitch in the Matrix everyone was dancing around, jailing at their best. That's why I was happy to sequester myself off into my cell and get my feelings on paper before they dissipated back into my present reality.

There are times in prison when I felt like I was watching everything take place from outside my own skin, not really being connected to the present. This was the first of those feelings that screamed in my head, "How the hell am I here?" It was not a pleasant or altogether enjoyable time. I thought about my upbringing, my education, and my morals. In all my life I never imagined being locked up in a cage like this, yet here I was. My only recourse was to figure out how to quickly adjust.

I entered back into the H Pod housing unit and immediately I could smell a hint of crazy in the air. Like there was a fire somewhere that I couldn't see. Guys were moving around juking and jiving, and there was a TV on full blast that nobody was watching, yet I could tell that it would be suicide to touch it or adjust the volume. The door leading out to the hallway locked behind me and I was back inside.

I felt tense. Guys were glancing at me since I was new, and I also had just left the pod to attend a Bible study. Never mind that my ultimate goal at first was to simply go to this churchy event so I could get out of our unit for a change of scenery. I had already seen what happened when inmates left the unit for a small while. They were talked about, plotted against, and belittled by a grade school of grown men. Oftentimes, they considered that the inmate had left to go talk to the Feds about becoming an informant and ratting guys out for a reduced sentence. Sometimes the inmate who left the unit was requesting to change to another pod since he felt unsafe. Regardless, the rumor mill was always on tilt, and the multitudes of these worries were running through my head now. All their suspicious eyes were on me and drawing conclusions about my character in a few rabid seconds.

Guys in these holding facilities are not usually genuine. We were locked up in small spaces, and everyone was worried about their upcoming sentences. It's like a pressure cooker, and you never know when someone is going to let out a burst of steam or who the unfortunate collateral damage will be. I was preparing for something to happen. To get pushed from behind, punched in the chest, or tripped. These are the ways I watched other inmates get jumped in my first several days in this place, so I figured it was only a matter of time until I became a target. All of these concerns flashed through my brain in a matter of seconds. I was too green to draw from experience; I had only the knowledge of what I'd seen recently. I made a brisk walk toward my cell for the perceived comfort of my bunk.

This is when I got a dose of schooling from a fellow inmate. He was a white guy with a shaved head and SS bolted tattoos on his *chest who happened to be my bunkmate at the time. Shep was my "cellie" as we called it. He started driving at me a little about where I went, why I needed to go to a prayer group, and that it was for weak-minded individuals who needed a crutch. His words were a big letdown after my enlightening experience at the prayer group, and again I began to realize that in prison there was going to be a lot of this. I was going to have to start standing up for myself continually until people learned to understand and accept me for who I was.*

Because my last name is long, and I happened to have requested kosher meals at my intake, he accused me of being Jewish. There was no logic behind his disputes. It seemed humorous at first until I realized that he wasn't fond of Jews, although Jews were better than blacks, he tells me. Mexicans aren't so bad either he says, but Jews he didn't know much about, only that they were different than himself, somehow. He continued on with this subject for several minutes trying to see how I would react or if I would be offended. I just sat there listening to him, trying to figure him out and to see if we were going to get along.

After getting a grip on the situation at hand, we talked it out for a little while. Following 10 minutes or so of questioning, he claimed to accept me since I was one of the few white guys in our pod and we needed to stick together. I tried to explain to him that I wasn't Jewish and that I got the kosher meals because they were healthier than the other crap they usually served us here. His response was that I had the mannerisms of Woody Allen and my glasses made me look Jewish. Even though I found this somewhat humorous, I could feel the tension of the situation, so I continued to calmly talk things out with Shep, not showing offense or anger to his accusations.

In my newfound interest with faith, literally from less than an hour ago, I decided to impart some hope to him about scripture. Quickly I realized I wasn't qualified to be doing so, but it felt like the right thing to do because of my enthusiasm. Somehow it diffused the situation, and we soon found ourselves on the same page with each other. We chatted for the rest of the evening up until lockdown at 10 p.m. I certainly appreciated the opportunity to bond with another human being there in that place.

Over our months in the holding facility, we became good pals. He helped me out by showing me the ropes and letting me know what to expect when I moved on to other places throughout my sentence. I spent my first birthday, Thanksgiving, and Christmas in prison sitting next to him eating chow and listening to him talk about how to cope with living through the holidays while being locked up. He was certainly a blessing, the first of many along the way. It's the nuggets of knowledge that he imparted during my first months in jail that helped me walk my time down and get through some thoroughly apprehensive years. Sheppard, I hope you are doing well out there, brother.

Some of the men I met at this, the inception of my chunk of time I was about to do, started to resemble people I knew before I had come to this place. These individuals were characters for sure. They each, in their own way, had exchanged a walk-on part in the real world for their own proclaimed lead role in this cage we now resided in. Each man strived upward in life to get something more. Generally, people don't end up in prison by accident. They must have sought out some objective in life, for better or worse, that was different from the manner in which they presently lived. It usually boiled down to money or drugs or both and was most likely not a well-thought-out plan of action. Therefore, a person traded normalcy in the world, a regular walk-on part, for a lead role in this new compressed version of the world, separate from reality. In this new lead role, they were the star of their own life's movie and could create whatever new character they wanted to be in there. I had to quickly learn to read people for liars or stand-up guys. If they were really who they said they were, or if I was about to be taken advantage of. With this in mind, I took reform into my own hands and was careful with whom I sought counsel.

From these people, I learned it was especially important to adjust strongly and assimilate smoothly—being quick to recognize who were full of shit, who were good influences, and if a guy was just saying whatever he felt necessary at the moment to make his time easier. I experienced it over and over where two inmates would have a conversation filled with lies and crap, and they probably both knew it. They would talk at length about where they had been, who they were with, and what they had done to get put in prison. They also discussed what facilities they had been in during their sentences—striving for credibility as if to beef up their resumes for a job interview. Mostly exaggerations, but all interesting stories to impress the other party. I, for one, got sick of listening to the other guys tell me stuff that I knew wasn't true. I'd sit there thinking "this guy must think I'm an idiot if he thinks I believe these flimsy stories," and I'd lose respect for them really quick.

When I was at my first holding facility, I remember a guy named B.W. talking to me about getting beat up by the correctional officers when they would move him for his recreation time. He claimed that the guards would come to his unit and announce that rec hour was available to anyone who wanted to attend. He would line up to leave, and then as he was led down the hallway to another chamber, the guards would open up a door and put him in a room where a handful of other inmates were participating in their rec time. He claimed, though, that it was a fight fest in this room. Guards and inmates all fist-fighting and brawling. Like it was some kind of fight-club gambling ring for the jailers.

He was really just trying to get me nervous during my first few weeks in jail, but this was typical of the type of conversations I had to deal with on a daily basis. They all just desired to incite fear and anxiety in others as a form of entertainment. Soon it became annoying that there weren't more normal conversations in there, only random, fake-sounding, one-sided conversations that wore me out. So I tried to avoid such nonsense. But it was difficult in our compressed living quarters.

This is also where nuggets of hope would shine through to me time and time again. I could tell if a man was truly God-centered because he wasn't full of crap. He would be humble, truthful, loving, and strong all at the same time, and it would be like a fresh breath of life. Experiencing this clarity once again proved that God was still with me in this walk, and He would get me through by continually putting good people in front of me and giving me the opportunity to grow and help others grow in turn. It was these glimmers of hope that would keep me going. God had quickly taught me to pay attention to people if I was going to get through this new life of mine and adhere to my self-imposed reform that was to be my curriculum in this school of hard knocks.

So right away, God spoke to me loud and clear. Whether it be the prayer group that got me out of my cell for an hour in Osceola, or my first cellmate at this same jail, it took being taken out of society for Him to get my full and undivided attention, and I am thankful that it happened like it did. If the situation were easier and more tolerable, I would have simply continued on with the scams, games, and hustles that surrounded me, since that is what I had been involved in during the years before my incarceration. It took hurt and despair to shake up my world and see the light that was just barely starting to shine on me, but boy did it ever continue to grow the more attention I gave my newfound spiritual hope. You just never know how or why things change in life, but if you learn to trust in the energy of the universe, which is love, then worry can harm you no more.

One of the few smiles in my first few years in prison. This photo was taken during my time in transit before I made it to Leavenworth. It's hard to tell that I was weary and searching my soul for relief.

Blessed to have a solid group of ladies visit me at Leavenworth Prison Camp. From left to right, mom Cheryl, cousin Jacquelyn, Corbin, Aunt Teri, Aunt B–Kay, Grams Pat.

It was good friends, like this crew pictured here, that I avoided as I started to deal drugs and do drugs at a harmful pace.

THE ONLY BREAK WE WOULD GET

"Dreams are that thought which has no end."
—Kohli

Early on in my prison sentence I observed an inmate wake up another inmate from a nap, and things did not end well for the instigator. While I was housed in the Forrest City Federal Correctional Complex (a low-security facility), I was living in an open-dorm setting. One of my nearby bunkmates, we'll call him EZ, was involved in the hustle of selling hand-rolled cigarettes for 10 stamps each. It wasn't easy to get this sort of contraband into a federal facility, but it was steady enough for this guy to have regular customers. Smoking isn't permitted in federal prison, but it is a regular occurrence. People like their nicotine and nursing a habit in a controlled environment can be a tricky endeavor.

Anyhow, on this occasion the distributor of said cigarettes was taking a nap in the middle of the day. One of his regular customers, we'll call him Dub, walked up to his bunk and began tapping on the sleeping man's shoulder. He must have felt quite comfortable in their relationship to do such a thing, but I soon learned that waking a man in prison is a poor activity to be involved in.

EZ quickly sat up, startled and visibly perturbed. He immediately open-hand slapped the cigarette seeker twice across the face and verbally berated him for several minutes. It was so loud that it attracted a crowd. Dub pleaded his case, exclaiming that he wanted to smoke at the next move (a 10-minute period where inmates could move between buildings around the facility) and that it would be count time soon (which meant that we would be locked down while they counted the entire inmate population by hand).

A few of his buddies swarmed the scene and quieted him down so he wouldn't alert the guard on duty. As quickly as the situation heated up, it subsided. The two gentlemen seemed to come to terms with each other, although EZ still had a look of disgust on his face.

So, he decided to sell him the cigarette that was so desired, and they both walked into the shower room to run the water as cover. There they lit up.

I wasn't in the shower with them to see it, but I heard a commotion in the stalls which was unmistakably the sound of a man getting jumped and beaten up. It only lasted 20 seconds or so. Then the men all exited the shower stalls, Dub looking battered and bruised.

Nothing was said after the incident, and it seemed as if everyone learned their lesson from it. I do recall, though, seeing a red mark on Dub's forehead a few days later, right in the dead center. It was the mark of a cigarette being extinguished, a cue how not to approach the cigarette hustler for a smoke. A reminder not to wake a sleeping man in prison.

###

It is a prudent practice in prison to not bother a man while he's sleeping. Unless it is count time or an officer is asking for this person specifically, then it's best to simply let a sleeping man lie. Being asleep is the only time one can be somewhere else, wherever his mind will take him. The thing about prison is that you are always there. The same hallways. The same people. The same attitudes. When you can get a nap or restful night's sleep, then it is a joyful thing, like visitation day or holiday-meal day.

My dreams were never more memorable than while in prison. It was an astonishingly wonderful surprise and became a secret that I wanted to keep to myself. I would fall asleep and remember places I had been before, like my camping trips to the north woods of Canada or kayaking excursions in the Sea of Cortez. It was as if I got to take these vacations again and experience the fun and excitement of being there. The dreams would occur in slow motion as I remembered details, during my slumber, that I could never have resurrected in my waking hours. It was the dullness of everyday life in jail which sparked such enjoyment that I took from these dreams. I would look forward to evening count every night with anticipation and curiosity of where I'd visit that night during my snoozing visions.

A favorite recurring dream that I had at least several times a month for several years involved my ex-girlfriend Emma, with whom I'd been seriously involved up until the time I was incarcerated. During these wonderful dreams, I became consciously aware of my body being asleep and then my spirit or soul leaving my body to visit people I missed the most. Usually, it was this treasured ex-girlfriend. Overnight I would float my way to Kansas City and show up at her condo to hang out with her for a few hours. She was aware of my presence there also, and she appreciated that I had left prison temporarily in my dream to visit her. It was a way for me to have closure with our separation. I missed her tremendously, and these dreams of us trying to repair our relationship were proof to me of that. It became a way for me to cope with the fact that I had lost her due to my previous noncommitted behavior and now my lack of presence in her life. These were great memories that would sustain me for days while wandering back and forth through the same hallways at Leavenworth.

As our time together in each of these dreams came near to a close, I would get anxiety about getting back to my sleeping body before I had to wake up, so I wouldn't be late getting back to prison. I didn't want to get in trouble for "escaping." As crazy as it sounds, it was a fun encounter for me and a nice little secret I kept over the years. It sounded too bizarre to share with anyone else, and it would probably have raised a lot of questions about my sanity if I had decided to share my clandestine endeavors with the other inmates.

I cherished my relationship with Emma, I really did. I also messed up repeatedly with her. She was loving and gentle, and I often ignored her requests to spend time together. It didn't start like that, but over the course of several years I put my illegal activities ahead of her love. From a bird's-eye view it's easy to see that prolonged drug use deteriorated my wits, judgement, and finally my actions with those close to me.

My upbringing taught me to respect women in relationships, and I always put forth a gallant effort to please any significant other in my life. There were some hits and misses, just like many people have in their young attempts at love. I noticed, though, that the more I started using substances as a social crutch that my decision-making suffered in turn. There were countless dreams where I would replay events from my past and try to rectify them by not being high or drunk. Then I would make a more astute decision in order to keep moving in a more positive direction. This made me feel as if I were repairing my life's mistakes, patching and updating the software in my biological CPU.

There was a recurring situation that I recall trying to correct in my dreams many times over the course of my prison sentence. Early on in my years of drug dealing I dated a sweet Puerto Rican girl named J. She was attracted to me because of the fast life that I lived and the exciting late evenings we spent romping around Kansas City with our friends. Happy hour martini bars, early morning electro music at clubs, margaritas on the decks of Plaza restaurants, and day-drinking on Sundays were all part of our early relationship's activities. It was exciting, and we surrounded ourselves with people who ran as hard as we did.

About six months into our relationship, she desired more. Instead of flashy extravagances, she wanted my time more than anything. I had started getting deeper into doing drugs and in turn moving drugs to subsidize my use and income. Our lives weren't exciting and new. I was lying to her about my whereabouts, I was constantly late to see her and taking her presence in my life for granted—everything contrary to how I was raised. Choosing to be in that world was changing my personality, and I was acting like a shadow version of myself.

Over the course of this particular bad week, I remember telling her that I would be at her house after she got off work. Each day I ignored my promise to her and continued running around the city. Monday turned into Thursday. It was a blur to me, but to her it was four consecutive days that I lied to her and never showed up at her apartment to spend time with her. One day she asked me to stop by the store and bring the ingredients for dinner home so she could cook for me. Another day she had tickets for us to go to a cultural food festival held in River Market, only blocks from where she lived. After each of her offers I told her I would be there and that we would have a wonderful evening. Every day that week I no showed her and decided instead to spend time dealing drugs and getting high. I chose to be around people who were virtual strangers instead of building a relationship with a nice girl who cared and was putting effort into us.

On Friday of that week everything came to a head. I promised J that I would be at her place with a bottle of wine so we could relax after her busy day at work. Our plans were to do whatever she wanted to do that evening so I could make up for being absent all week and ignoring her. Well, at 5:30 when I was supposed to be at her place, I was still in my car running drug errands. I hadn't lost track of time; I just simply didn't care. Being on drugs can make a person numb to actual responsibilities in life. So, as I was busy avoiding my girlfriend, I found myself driving around downtown Kansas City with another girl in the passenger seat of my car. I barely knew this young female, and the only reason she was with me was to be close to the drugs I was harboring. She was kind of cute, so I thought it was fun be-bopping around town with her as a sidekick. Actually, this was a hugely disrespectful and irresponsible thing to do. I knew deep down it was not cool, but I wasn't in my right mind with the long week of drugs flowing steadily through my body.

As I was driving around that afternoon I ventured downtown, near where J lived. I wasn't paying attention to which neighborhood I was in until I stopped at a stop sign and looked up. There *stood J out on a walk with her dog. Her phone was to her ear and I could feel my phone vibrating in my pocket. Karma had caught up to me and I was caught red-handed being a complete fool. Served me right, but it certainly wasn't fair to J. Anyhow, you can probably imagine this was the beginning of the end of my relationship with J, and rightfully so. It was a horrible way to cap off a rude and crude week of ignoring her. She saw me driving around with some random gal while I was dealing drugs. Just a poor choice of living on my part. My life was a mess at that point, and anyone meaningful suffered because of my hair-brained behavior.*

So now that you know the outline of my fallout with J, here is what happened numerous evenings while I was asleep and working through my dreams in prison. This situation in particular was one that I dreamt about many times. Each time I would try and correct my behavior throughout the week, giving myself a better chance at resurrecting my relationship with J and making things right in my life again. I relived this week many times in my dreams, and this was my version of a Groundhog Day where I knew my dreamtime was temporary, but it was still healing to my soul. I think that for me it was real, and in a sense, it was truly healing in those restorative dreams. I never really got to make it up to J in the real world, but in our spiritual realm I do believe that she forgave me and that we were nurtured through our efforts to heal. This healing process I created for my dreamtime practices was just another way to make the years behind bars more meaningful to my existence.

These dreams were also proof to me that our minds and bodies are restorative and want healing if we only allow it to happen. When we permit ourselves to accept our mistakes and we forgive ourselves for making them, our foundations are strengthened and our life's meaning becomes deeper and more colorful.

As important as these dreams were to me at that time in my life, it is our aspirations that keep us moving on to the next event in our own lives. These ambitions are usually centered on temporary desires and urges like hunger, sex, comfort, and excitement. The object of our own affections can be fleeting and confusing in the sense that we really don't know what is important to us in life's larger sense. The main question I started to ask myself was this: Was I involved in what is important to our existence in the larger purpose of the universe? Was I doing what I am meant to do in life?

I recalled a T-shirt that I bought back in Lawrence, Kansas that had a picture of a Rastafarian man on the front of it and a revealing quote on the back. I was a first-year college student and quite eager in my search for ways to expand my mind's eye. The shirt stated, *The object of nature is man. The object of man is soul.* What a great way this T-shirt was to establish my own identity back then. It was a nonverbal way to let others know that by reading my shirt you could catch a glimpse of what was going on in my mind and what I stood for in life.

I may not have completely comprehended what I stood for at the time, but I knew that I was a radical thinker and believed in something larger than myself that was helping me through this life. An understanding gradually developed that if we are for our soul and our soul is for God, then we are for God. If we remember to stay God-centered, then all the temporary desires of life will simply fall into place and therefore happiness will fall into place. It sounded a little simplified, but it was the best way I had to rationalize my existence while spending years waiting my release.

Through some of the dreamtime sessions I had during my sentence in the Bureau of Prisons, I came to understand various things about life that kept me feeling connected to something larger than myself. Along with these understandings arose a firm grip on my beliefs concerning our existence. Generally, I formed this belief in my head with the understanding that it didn't contradict my beliefs in God or my acceptance of science. Atoms lead to energy, energy leads to spirit, and spirit leads to God. Vibrations spawning from God (souls) became individual and separate from the universe source. This separation ended the state of perfection (being one with God) and can be equated to the revolt of the angels or the fall of man. In turn, this can be how the idea of evil, darkness, worldly ways, and sin came about. The more spiritually connected I became, the more I strived to accept our place in the universe. The minute we became human we became imperfect, not of God anymore. The spirit of God pushed itself into matter (physical) and became man. From the supernatural beauty of the universe to the physical plane as we know it. The evolution of pure light to matter. Father, Son, and Holy Spirit. We are the Holy Spirit, and the Holy Spirit is us and in us. It is our connection back to God, the Creator, the all living being.

This is how the evolution of the soul can happen. When a person can still their mind and just be in the time of their life that they are living presently, then pure life is occurring.

As I first learned to simply not disrupt a sleeping man in prison, I soon came to appreciate the power of dream life and had a whole new respect for this practice. The mind is the builder of the individual entity. When you open your mind to receive the light and grow in the spirit of the universe, you open your mind to be within God's will for you and your being.

This is the struggle in life—that all souls belong to God but are suffering because they are separate, just like being separated from your family, yearning to be back with them again. It is these struggles that enable the soul to grow, evolve, and actually become closer to God. A strange paradox isn't it? We all belong together, we function better and are happiest, best, and complete when we are together. If we can cope with and finally embrace being separate and become stronger individually while separate, it makes being together all the more glorious and whole. Togetherness is light, and light is the source of life. Life is being in and with universal happiness, enlightenment. Each life evolves each soul forward (or in some cases backward) to eventually get back to God. We are all finding our way back to where we came from, and the comparison of sleep being a break from life in prison really humbles the idea of soul evolution and makes it more approachable and understandable.

So at this point, my goal has been to impress upon you my feelings as to why dreams are important. These beliefs came to me over the years of my imprisonment, sparked from listening to other inmates' advice to not wake another man while he was sleeping and from reading various books while fitting their subjects into the construct of my mind's understanding and beliefs.

The dreams also had sources dating all the way back to the days of buying T-shirts to express myself in college. Dreams can make our lives feel all the grander and give us a sense of wonder and splendor that is often fleeting in fixed living. I remember I would dream in my younger years, as a child and adolescent. I know I had hope for the future. I'm also sure that I would have dreamt in my 20s, but for some reason those memories are clouded and unsure. The fog created by trying to live life in the fast lane and chase vanity led to a blunted dreamlife and limited spiritual life. Therefore, my true meaning for living was not happening and my days were dismal and grey.

I yearned for the clarity of my younger years of growing up in that small rural town in Kansas. Hunting after worldly desires and passing urges got the best of me after college. "Chase that dollar," I said to myself. "Work hard but play harder," I repeated daily. Then what soon followed were my attempts to figure out how to fit into a socially scalable crowd to boost my own status. Finally, when I spread my heart in so many directions that there was nothing left except a brittle foundation, I was ripe for ruin. Constantly making decisions based on pleasing others to keep that social standing was tiresome and unrewarding. There was no time for self-reflection, only personal tragedy. Learning to appreciate dreams has become restorative and forgiving.

If you are ever dreaming, learn to cultivate your time there and enjoy it for what it is. Understanding dream life isn't important right away, and if you desire to delve deeper into dream meanings, then there are books for that, and they are interesting indeed. Usually, the idea that your dreams are speaking to you can be a good sign that your life is evolving forward and that you are living in the purpose of your meaning for God. This should be enough to make you happy and exude love to others. Remember, spreading love in the world only brings up the level of positive intimacy between humans as spiritual beings and in turn aims us toward a happier world.

Learning to love the nighttime dreams we have can turn out to be utterly amazing. Think about dreams in terms of aspiration. The goals we have in life. Where we see ourselves 10 years from now. Often our desires turn to worldly wants, such as a house, car, job, money, and lover. Well, it's good to have these goals, but we must also remember that God has perfect timing and things in our lives happen as they are supposed to. Our life's plan is unfolding just as God intended it, and if you believe in that, then you'll always be comfortable and content.

But you want more than content. You want exciting and adventurous. You want dazzling and glamorous. You want notoriety and credit for all your accomplishments, and you want people to notice and respect you for being such a high-value human being and soldier in this world.

Well, I can tell you how this turned out for me and how we got to this point right now. I am typing on a laptop in my mom's kitchen after just being let out of federal prison on work release. I'm on a six-month home-confinement program where I only leave to go to work at a local lumberyard (Mark II Lumber) and to shop at the local Walmart. I sometimes get to go out to eat at a restaurant. When I do leave the house, I must drive a direct route and call to prove my present location. It is a slow time in my life, but it's giving me the opportunity to use my writing as therapy. As I type these words, my aim is to see if my experiences can touch someone else out there in a positive way. In these reflections, maybe someone else can veer in the direction of making better choices rather than giving in to greed or vanity.

Trying to please or impress others is a tiresome task. Years ago, I was chasing some more shallow dreams. I was reckless, and here is what happened one night while looking for success in all the wrong places.

In 2009, I was in the middle of moving quantities of drugs around Kansas City and living what I considered the high life on

60

The Country Club Plaza. I was chasing that so-called dream of money and popularity while subsequently nursing a drug habit that was worthy of a wide-range social experiment.

I would spend my days meeting up with this person or that person, gathering certain pills or money. I would then find a way to trade for cocaine so I could spin that off into getting a car or other large ticket item. I could then turn around and sell it for thousands more. I thought it was fun, this game I liked to play with illegal substances, and I convinced myself for years that I was growing a business for myself. The continual hustle that I thought would get me to a certain station in life where I would have respect and a feeling of accomplishment was slowly tearing at my soul and leaving me more and more empty as the days passed. This striving for what I thought were my dreams in life was actually a total fluke, and I was fooling myself into thinking I had a plan and that it was working.

How wrong I was.

For years I was creeping around to different houses throughout the days where people were waiting on me so we could do business. The feelings I had of being in control of their time, money, and addictions were a high for me just as much as the drugs were. There would be calls from people about having a rendezvous in the public parking lot of a grocery store or a hidden alley in Midtown. Listening to what they wanted and then striving to fulfill their need like an ambitious salesman was exhilarating, and I convinced myself that I was doing a service to those in need. Crazy, huh? The things we'll do to make ourselves feel as though we are veracious and that we are simply reaching for our life's goals and dreams.

The key to remember here is that it wasn't one decision that got me down this path, this rabbit hole that was eroding my life and my character. It was many small decisions over the course of time that finally ended in a judge-ordered "time out" behind bars. A 90-month federal prison sentence.

There were several times in the midst of those years that I had moments of clarity and knew I had to change what I was doing, but these instances were brief, as there was always someone there to lead me back to the dark side. In this memory, I was in the middle of shuttling a chunk of cocaine probably worth several thousand dollars across to the other side of the Plaza in the middle of a snowstorm. For some reason, it stands out in my mind because I remember the efforts I extended to get this particular deal done. A bunch of people were holed up for the night in a nice house nearby and they were looking to make their night a little zippier. We exchanged some texts, and after a few hours I convinced myself to make my way over there. I gathered up my things and bundled up for the drive. It was normally only a five-minute jaunt, but I had no idea what the hills and ice would have in store for me that night. It had been cold and snowing for hours by now.

The darkness outside quieted the still-early evening as I headed out to my car. I noticed there were no other vehicles on the streets. Great, nobody to pull me over for swerving all over the roads if they happened to be slick. No other cars to impede my progress or to watch out for.

I got into my Benz and put my little satchel in its hiding place, a magnetic compartment hidden underneath my driver's seat. During this whole process, my phone was making all sorts of noise. My little robot that was in charge of my life. It was the people calling to ask how much longer I would be, my girlfriend texting me asking why I wasn't responding to her, and my family texting me wondering if I was alright in this storm. I was bundled up with gloves, a stocking cap, and it was exceedingly difficult to use my phone while trying to drive. I do remember my frustration level had started to rise. It is always the anxiety of the work that I remember. All I could think of was that I had to fulfill the need, the request of something that these people wanted, like a good salesperson would. Like a good businessman. I had convinced myself that I was being smart and ambitious at my job.

The drive over to this house was foolish, with the wind and the snow blowing and the roads barely visible. The streetlights that were usually helpful in illuminating the roads were now blurry and confusing. The electronic music that streamed through my car's speakers was sketching out my brain to the point of second guessing my decision to jump into this mess. I impatiently tapped the steering wheel and scooted along until I was near the intersection where the house and these people were. With all the distractions, I would be pleased when this drive was over and done. It was mentally taxing and had worn me out in a matter of 10 minutes.

I recall blinking my eyes constantly and turning them in circles. Rolling and darting them around to keep my composure. It was an attempt to control the chemicals flowing through my veins. The combination of ingesting and selling the drugs was aging me quicker than my young life should have shown. Often the thoughts of a heart attack or a mental breakdown weighed on my brain. But I had to pull myself together. There was work to do and my services were needed.

Luckily, I was able to find a parking spot nearby, so I skidded in, turned my car off, and gathered my things. My phone was still making all sorts of racket; I would address that issue when I got inside. The snow and wind all around was dizzying. How in the world did I make it over here in the first place? I found myself asking questions like that more often as my drug use increased over the years. A thought that used to run through my head was, "I gotta remember not to get high while I'm out doing this crap."

Making my way to the front door, I was eager to step inside and take a few minutes to warm up. It was important to get my bearings straight again if I were to get any business done. I was a bit shaken from this whole experience, and I just wanted to get on with things. The minute I stepped in, I was bombarded with all sorts of questions. What took me so long? Is the product any good? Why was there snow all over me? Did I want to stay and party? My only response was to throw them the bag that they desired and wait for the money so I could get back to my safe, warm home.

So I did just that. I mentioned how much money they owed me a few times. I reminded them that I still had to drive home and that it would be good to get going while I was still bundled up. Instead, they got busy right away doing their drugs, ignoring my request for money and desire to leave. That's when it hit me like a bag of wet spaghetti. A heavy, wet, slimy slug of reality. It was the first time that I recall contemplating my rank in life and how the events and choices over the year had led to this. Weary, pathetic, and altogether ate up—I knew it was all my own doing. It was a nauseating feeling to have this all culminate right now.

Memories of playing high school sports and getting ice cream with pretty girls after school crossed with my present situation of delivering drugs around the Plaza. It was too much for me to contemplate, and my head began to tighten. All I wanted to do was get back home and deal with my problems alone. My anxious mind was making me nervous and sad all at once.

Then a guy said two things to me that started my mind off into a direction of clarity and discontent.

He first asked why it was always such a task to get the drugs that he wanted in a timely fashion? Why couldn't it be like a pizza delivery or a stop into the local grocery store? I had to calmly remind him that these substances are illegal and that there are a lot of logistical hoops one must go through to get them and distribute them. I was getting pretty angry by now but kept my cool because there was still the formality of getting paid for my efforts in this transaction.

Then the second question came out of his mouth. He said, "How about you front me this and I'll get you the two grand next weekend?" Well, that made my eyes start to boil; I should have been prepared for something like this. How stupid was I to not get these details all straightened out before making this hairy drive over here? I was mad at myself, peeved at these guys, and stressed about having to drive back home in this damn blizzard. What was going on in my life that I had ended up in this situation? Did I need all this? Is this what my life had become? This current situation had proven to me that drug dealing wasn't as glamorous or exciting as I had thought in previous years. Was I now supposed to be a tough guy or a pushover? Should I play the part of the person who was going to be cool with it all and simply live for the moment? I couldn't conceive of how I had let my life get to this point, and now it was all festering up in fear, anger, and even a little melancholy.

That is when I became lucid and fully aware. What a mess this all was, the whole thing. Not just this faulty blizzard drug deal gone awry, but my life. The entire existence I had created for myself. This wasn't me at all, but here I was living it and seeing it unfold right before my eyes. Here and now was not the life I had dreamed mine would be. I was not living out my goals of making money and gaining respect. I wasn't living a childhood dream of working at a magazine developing content for stories about outdoor gear. I wasn't some fabulous advertising salesman exceeding his monthly quota. No, this was something else entirely. This was a no-money and no-respect situation that was about as far from enjoyable as a person could get.

I missed my family. I missed my girlfriend. I missed my life, and I missed my calling that God had intended for me, because I tried to do things my way, the way of the world. All matters considered, I decided to wrap up my session at this place. Gathering what little money I could from these lame dudes, I left to make the drive back to my house so I could simply stay in for the rest of the evening and think about getting my life back in order.

Upon exiting their house, I noticed how the snowstorm was still in full gush and the roads were actually bordering on dangerous. After my car started, I let it warm and started pulling back out onto the road toward my house. In a matter of a few seconds, I was spinning all over the place with no traction in this fluffy powder. The stress of the situation was really starting to get at me, and I was nearing panic-attack mode. Things being as they were, I was sliding and spinning in the snow, but mostly I was just stuck in the middle of this intersection only 20 feet from where I'd been parked. Frustrated, feeling crappy, cold, and hopeless. There were no other cars out that night, so help was hard to come by.

It took me over two hours to get back home in numerous fits of pushing my car, rocking it back and forth, and just flooring it through intersections while only actually moving at a few miles an hour. This event, incidentally, got me thinking about all the big stuff. How did I get here? How was I to turn things around? How was I going to get my life righted when I couldn't even get this car going forward in the right direction without swerving all over the street and banging on the steering wheel? There I sat, screaming at the top of my lungs with nobody around to hear. It was a lonely existence, and looking back at it now, I am even more scared knowing that I wasn't recognizing God in my life during that period of struggle.

The magnificent thing is, He was there and hadn't given up on me. In that moment, He was speaking to me, and I somehow knew it but failed to act on His request to seek Him out and live for His purposes. Years later when I finally got my act together, I became fond of what is now one of my favorite verses in the Bible. It would have served me well that day in the storm, had I been more aware of what it meant. Romans 8:28 states that "all things work for the good of those who love God and that are called according to His purposes." Remembering to be in line with God's will works for the good in my life? What an extraordinary way to live! How fulfilling and comfortable it is to know that loving God and living for His will in our lives brings happiness and joy to us and those around us.

With the benefit of hindsight, it's now easy to see how all these small bad choices along the way got me into that snowstorm, away from God's will in my life. The great thing is, it's also easy to see how so many good choices since then returned me back within His will for my life and back to happiness. It's a warming feeling to know that we are never too far gone to find our way back into His loving arms. We are always one good decision away from gaining goodness back into our lives. It only takes the belief that we are unique and have meaning larger than ourselves in this world. Our next action in life will either draw us closer to our purpose or push us away from it. We need not change the whole world all at once to make our lives meaningful; we need only to do the next right thing according to His calling.

Dreams, we all have them, and they are a blessing in life, be it the kind that are our goals for ourselves personally or the type that we live through during our hours of sleep. I learned not to wake a sleeping man and not to live for the worldly dreams that are fleeting. Live for the dreams that we are meant for and they will surely come true in ways that you never thought possible. Trust in what God has in store for you, and then go out and live every day by treating others with love and respect and in turn receiving it. Sometimes it may take being humbled, hurt, or even scared to wake you up to the ways of our purposes here in this life. But whatever your moment of clarity, embrace it and make the next right thing happen in your life. Then spread the positivity.

*The evidence of my troubling past choices are a reminder of where
I came from and how to positively proceed for a renewed and
wonderful life.*

My grandmother faithfully wrote me every week of my 64 months in prison. This is her birthday in 2019.

MEN ARE BITCHES

"Whatever is begun in anger ends in shame."
—Benjamin Franklin

Every stop in the BOP had its own rules when it came to visitation. Sure, there was a guidebook of specific policies and procedures for inmates and administrators to follow, but it was the unwritten code of conduct that was adhered to first. Oftentimes, different prison guards at each place enforced their own dress code. This made visitation day in prison stressful for everyone—inmates, visitors, and guards included. Some places demanded that visitors' shirts be tucked in. Others didn't care if shirts were tucked in at all, as long as the shirt was plain and generic with no visible logo. Short sleeves were frowned upon, but in the dead of summer it was hot, so they changed the standard for a few months. Sometimes this standard would drift into the winter months until one day they remembered it was a rule again and there were no short sleeves allowed. Not now, not ever. Too much skin showing.

Certainly, visitors were not allowed to wear short skirts. That would just make sex-deprived inmates too excited. Until one day there was this beautiful woman who came through with a short tight skirt around her legs and fancy sunglasses atop her flowing hair. The younger girl with her (probably her college-aged daughter) had white yoga pants on, clinging to her like wet rubber. The guard on duty that day was probably drooling over these two attractive ladies and decided to bend the rules. The inmate population all stared like fools and talked about it for days to come. We would get pretty bored in the joint, so this was great fodder for dinner conversation. Those two girls probably got eye-molested more than a few times that afternoon during their prison visit.

No sunglasses were allowed either, but I often saw people with them stuck on the top of their head like this skirt-wearing MILF did that day. At one point during my sentence, my personal eye-glasses broke, and I remembered that lady from months earlier with the fancy outfit. So I hatched a plan for my brother to wear a pair to our next visit so he could hand them off to me.

At the next visit with my brother, he wore some glasses bearing my prescription on his head. At one point, he took them off and set them on the table in front of me. After a few moments, I casually picked them up myself and placed them on my face. At the conclusion of the visit, I waltzed back into the prison with a new pair of specs. We didn't get caught, and my sight was better off for the successful caper.

Before I got the glasses from my brother, I wore my broken set that was cobbled together with some lame tape that I procured. I was forced to repair them with new tape several times a day. They were in pieces, and it was a rough month. He saved my butt, because it took the Bureau over a year to get me a pair of those ugly army issued glasses to use. In this instance, the visiting rules enforced by the BOP came in handy.

The rule was vague concerning who would be let in while wearing jogging or exercise pants. My friend Cristian and his wife Lisa drove all the way from KC to visit me while I was housed in Forrest City, Arkansas. After waiting for 45 minutes in line to get into the visiting room, Cristian was told that he couldn't wear the Adidas running pants he had on, so they made him leave and drive to Walmart and buy some regular jeans to wear to the visit. They were inconvenienced by the ordeal, and our visiting time was shortened by a few hours since they had to go shopping. There was no sign stating that running pants were not allowed. The sign only stated that short skirts and short pants were not allowed. The guards that day altered the dress code because one week earlier, a male visitor was getting a hand job by a male inmate at the visit. I suppose loose-fitting pants made this sort of activity more efficient. It's amazing the kind of antics we had to regularly put up with!

The visitors in my family learned to keep extra outfits in their cars just in case they were made to change. My grandmother wore the same clothes every time she visited so she was sure to be admitted. This was a safeguard to avoid her previous inconveniences.

On one visit, she was turned away for having wire framing in her bra; this was considered a hazard for some reason. She was returned to the rear of the line, giving her at least another 45-minute wait before a chance for entry would present itself. At the sight of what happened to my grandmother, other women ran off to the restroom. There they took off their bras (containing the same wire framing) and began to chew off the sides so they could cleverly remove the wires before they too would be dismissed to the back of the line. Some of the women threw their bras in the trash but immediately fished them back out.

They remembered that they wouldn't be allowed entry if they weren't wearing undergarments. My mother witnessed this in shock. It was like the guards were humiliating the visitors for being there to visit these lowly inmates. This resulted in the visitors being disgraced into dismantling or discarding their own undergarments to avoid being sent to the rear of the line.

It was like a circus every time I had people come to see me. Those who visit inmates housed in federal prisons get treated like cattle. They get talked down to, snarled at, and are given conflicting information from one visit to the next. Even from one person to the next. The administration claims it is for safety purposes, but there's no logic or merit in most of what they say. So there's a good portion of each visiting day that is consumed with the conversation of "... what the heck is really going on around here?" We were often asked by our families if people get treated like that regularly. There was a smattering of misguided information and haphazard direct orders. These orders were mixed with changing policies to fit the mood of the particular guard on duty. Our answer was always a resounding, "Yes, we are treated unfairly and often worse." One wouldn't consider that Americans would treat other Americans like this. My experiences have proven to me that going to a visit at a federal prison makes any TSA experience seem like a trip to an amusement park.

I was out of prison by the time COVID-19 became an issue in our country, and so I'm grateful for not dealing with the new issues that certainly tainted prison visitations in 2020. I even heard that inmate visitation days were suspended and postponed depending on the health regulations at that particular time. My guess is that it has only became trickier, just like the rest of the world.

###

So you think a male prison is filled with tough guys? Strong-minded men with type-A personalities that walk around with their chests puffed out and a chip on the shoulder? Dudes ready to throw down at the drop of a plastic spork in the chow hall or the mention of an ex-wife on the basketball court? Well, these stereotypes do ring true in federal prison, but there are also some other characteristics about prison that normal citizens would never realize.

Here's one thing that really surprised me. The guys I was around in prison (I was at nine different facilities in six years) complained more than any other people I have been around in my life. They would complain about the food, the bunks, the cramped quarters, not having money on their commissary, someone else who owed them money, their judge, their attorney, their sentence, other inmates, the stink of the toilets, or numerous other things that people with too much time on their hands would think of to complain about.

Indeed, these are all valid concerns while spending time locked up, and we all understand how misery loves company. Complaining and whining are what I recall most in the six years I was down, and I never got over it until I finally left the system and worked myself back into reality. But looking back from the outside in, I finally understand what all that complaining was really about and, more importantly, what the underlying theme to all the bitching was.

Many guys I came across in prison got sentences that seemed extremely long for who they were and what they had done to get themselves in there. Deep down these guys were not complaining about the conditions or other inmates. At the core of the bitching was the grief from missing their families because of the many years of being incarcerated. They were hurting from the burdens of having the male head of the family locked up for a decade or longer. Many guys got 10–15-year sentences because of small amounts of drugs. Mostly these drugs were to facilitate a habit formed because of an addiction, a disease ingrained into the psyche of those unfortunate enough to be born with it. The Feds will wrap up these small amounts of drugs into larger conspiracies to enable them to punish small time offenders to long sentences. This gives the prosecutors a feather in their cap for "cleaning up the streets" and "fighting the war on drugs." So, these men sit for years in prison and grumble about their situation. I've seen it, lived it, and been through the system myself. It's a shame and a drag on taxpayers, especially the working class.

Large-scale prison reform in the United States of America is long overdue. There has been small action taken at various times throughout the years, but it has mostly been a lot of talk generally leading to the furthering of agendas geared toward other political needs. Jared Kushner helped push some productive reform through at the end of 2018, but it will take some time to determine if any progress is made from its action. In mid-2019 some reform laws were passed to help reduce sentences by earning good time for federal inmates. The fear, though, is that by its implementation, dangerous individuals will be set free sooner than necessary. Many people who are conservative in nature (not necessarily Republicans) support laws to simply stay with the old practice of tough-on-crime initiatives rather than study and understand the affects that prolonged incarceration has on our society. The consequences run beyond the families that are directly related to those individuals actually doing the time. The more Americans that are put through the prison systems, the more of a grind it puts on our country as a whole. It creates a purposeful welfare around the families and friends of those who take the effort to support the loved ones who are in the midst of plodding through long, burdensome sentences.

After doing time in the federal system and hearing thousands of men complain about their hardships and suffering, I have come to two conclusions. One is that men are bitches. I have never been around so many grown men, tough guys, heads of families, fathers, husbands, brothers, and overall good dudes who whine and complain as much as in prison. It was astonishing and pathetic at times. It also made me sad and disappointed to see and hear it so regularly. When I first arrived at a federal prison, I was under the impression that I would enter a situation where men would be working together to pull each other through what can be considered some of the toughest years a person will endure in his life. There is support and guidance to an extent if you surround yourself with the right people, no doubt. But more than not, there is this feeling of dismay, regret, and a general jaded attitude toward authority and the government overall. This feeling seeps out to anyone who is in contact with these inmates, whether it be family who visits, friends who correspond by mail, or a significant other who puts money on an inmate's commissary account. They are all exposed to the rants and complaints about the crappy situation one must live through for the years of being locked up. Simple misery reaching out for any open ear that will hear its grievances, and I was part of the misery myself.

The second conclusion is this: These men are bitches for incredibly good reasons. As hard as it was for me to get used to hearing guys sound like complaining little weaklings, it is even more disheartening to see and hear US citizens treat and oppress other US citizens the way they do in prisons. To live in a place where respect is battled over every minute of every day is tiring. The tug of war where no man wants to budge on their stance and beliefs or show any empathy to others is apparent to everybody there. Guards, inmates, administrators, healthcare staff, prosecutors, whoever. It will erode a person down to where all that is left is a hardened shell of who they once were. The longer a person is there (inmate, guard, etc.), the more jaded he becomes until the real world seems so far away. Then it gets easier to join in on the bitching.

Nobody could have convinced me that US prisons are the way they are before I entered one. The average citizen assumes that they keep the bad people away from society for safety reasons and that they provide programs to help retool and improve those who are willing to accept help. The reality I found is definitely contrary to this. They are storage facilities, warehouses where people are the inventory. Each inmate is shuffled around for years as they wait out their sentence to completion. A few educational programs are available, but you have to be ambitious enough to seek them out, and then it is usually other inmates who facilitate them. The days are mostly made up of finding methods to keep the boredom at bay. This is why so many guys get involved in underhanded activities inside—nonsense type stuff that is mostly bad for the souls of those who are involved and anyone else who gets caught up in them.

So yes, there are some bad people in there, and prisons are necessary to keep repeat offenders off the street and away from hurting society any more than they already have. Certainly, these people need structure, discipline, and to be kept on a tight schedule in order to maintain a buttoned-up and tidy institution. But I was around so many men who could have been the average neighbor, co-worker, or friend and they were in the middle of doing five, six, some of them more than ten years for mistakes they made. Mind you, these guys were not criminal masterminds, but they messed up and made some bad decisions.

The amount of time that judges are handing out made me gasp over and over. The federal mandatory minimums were created to punish the worst of the worst criminals that were taking advantage of honest, hardworking Americans—crimes that were interstate oriented, such as drug trafficking across the country, racketeering, computer and internet related offenses, or crimes against the nation itself. Many of the guys I was around were low-hanging fruit that were snatched up for suspicious-looking but not altogether high-end activities. The Feds would then decide to pile up some charges and make these individuals sound much worse than they really were. The next thing these guys knew, they were caught up in a federal indictment where the charges dictated how much time they were given, and the judges really had no say in the matter. It's as if the federal prosecutors get to determine how much time the accused person will end up doing, and that is way too much power for any human to handle. I saw it firsthand, a prison industrial complex growing out of control like a slothful monster drunk on its own power and greed. Shameful.

So many of these guys either messed up at work while dealing with large amounts of money, were nursing a drug habit and found a way to fund this habit through sales of the product, or made some hasty business decisions that ended on the wrong side of legal. These are mistakes, mental-health issues, and outright bad decisions. This is not the work of devious criminals worthy of being treated like the dregs of society. These are not the types of mistakes that deserve the punishment of years on a compound away from families, separated for a decade or more. No second chances, no opportunities to help yourself out while in prison and earn some time back. Only the prospect of living under the heavy hand of a federal government whose ego is swiftly growing out of control. Judges acquiesce to prosecutors who seek long sentences with no regard to what they are doing to the fabric of our nation. The prosecutor basically recommends a sentence, and the judge goes along with this recommendation all while the population of our prisons grows and grows. The result is more and more people behind bars, adding to the drag on our society. Many of these inmates are decent Americans who simply let some bad decisions get blown out of proportion. The Department of Justice is so focused on convictions that they don't see how they are doing more harm than good in keeping our country safe. I thought that keeping our country safe was the sole purpose this agency was created for in the first place?

People wonder why there is aversion everywhere these days. Shootings at schools, angry middle-class workers, hopeless voters, and bipartisan hatred. How we treat each other in a court of law is a microcosm of how much respect is reciprocated in our society on a daily basis. When I started the process of going to court, I assumed that the respect I showed for the system and processes in place would work out in fairness for all parties involved. I never claimed I was innocent, I pleaded guilty in my case. I didn't understand why the Feds were piling on charges to try and give me more time than the crimes that were really committed would have given me. I figured they were just trying to make a tough case against me—but I assumed the truth would come out in the end. It was beyond me to believe that they would outright lie to try and beat me down. I trusted the system to be fair, accurate, and in everyone's best interests. I did this and so did the thousands of men I heard bitch about it for the six years I was in the federal prison system. We were bamboozled, and it is still happening to men and women every day. They are being torn away from their families, being treated like terrorists, and then warehoused in a system that neither accounts for well-being nor rehabilitation.

I was at several institutions, but only two for any length of time. One of these institutions was at Leavenworth, Kansas. A guy I knew at Leavenworth, we'll call him C.W., had a great quote that he would always pull out when guys were bitching too much. He would say, "If you wanted things to be easy, then you shouldn't have come to prison." Ironic. Nobody wants to be in prison, but there you sit, living a life that you would have never chosen for yourself, locked up.

C.W. was my cellmate for a year. He got a 10-year sentence for money laundering, a 10-year mandatory minimum because that is the way the federal guidelines are set up. He had good reasons to be jaded. C.W. got a call one day from the FBI asking if he had cashed some commission checks he received from the sale of some real estate. He told them yes, because that is how he got paid in his business of buying and selling properties. He would sell a property and take a small percentage commission for himself for brokering the deal. It happened every day all over our great country, capitalism at its best. But in this situation, he was informed that his commission check that he had deposited into his bank account was obtained from illegal

81

funds. C.W. had no intent of being involved in shady dealings. This was news to him, so he asked what needed to happen next? The agent explained that he was now under investigation for fraud.

Well, since C.W. felt that he had done nothing wrong, he wasn't too worried. Maybe he would be fined or would be ordered to straighten it out with the source of his commission income, but certainly he didn't feel he broke any laws and freely admitted he was willing to work with the FBI for the best possible outcome for everyone involved. He soon learned that the best possible outcome was not what the FBI had in mind. They only wanted to find as many people as they could and charge them with as many possible crimes as they could find, while getting these people caught up in a federal criminal system that would plague their lives for decades. The FBI threatened to put his wife and son in prison, as well, unless he pleaded guilty and took his lumps for the next 10 years in prison. It all happened so suddenly, and he didn't know what else to do, so he took his sentence like a man and has recently finished up his 10-year bit at Leavenworth.

This situation reminds me of an exercise practiced in law schools that I read about in several different sources over the years. An assignment would be given to the class on a Friday. The professor would assign the class a particular celebrity and tell them to research this person over the weekend. The research would consist of finding activities that seemed questionable or shady. Then the following week they would take this research and find as many crimes as possible to charge this celebrity with. The eager students would pigeonhole activities of these celebs to fit the qualities of a crime and even find ways to make assumptions on the part of these famous people to make their activities fit the crimes.

The purpose of this activity is to teach these aspiring lawyers to think outside the box and help them find ways to make those who are deserving punishment receive it. Unfortunately, it looks as if this exercise has spilled over into other areas of the criminal justice system and thusly taken on a life of its own. Read the book *Three Felonies a Day: How the Feds Target the Innocent*, by Harvey Silvergate, if you are interested in understanding this topic more. I simply wanted to reference it here to enlighten you on the mindset of those in the law arena.

Let me revisit the reasons I have complained about men who bitch constantly in prison. I recall how new inmates in the system would react to their living situation. Oh, how annoying newbies can be. After I had been in prison for several years already, I always hated hearing these new guys say, "I don't understand why…" and then end with something silly like, "… we have to tuck in our shirts to go into the chow hall." They would continue to complain that the rules weren't reasonable and that the guards were callous and senseless. I would often hear, "… don't they know who I am? I owned a business and was a member of my church and …" so on and so forth. It got to be very stereotypical and annoying to hear guys talk like they were somebody special or worse, like any of us cared about their dismay. We were all going through this tough mess together, nobody better, nobody worse than the next person. Yet repeatedly, there were guys bitching about the current conditions and making claims about how they were going to fix it.

It's amazing to see how people react when they are subject to an authority they cannot fight with much success. Well, they bitch. Grown men. They complain to anyone who will listen and look for others who will bitch with them. Now, with good reason these men bitch, because they have often been treated unfairly and are now in a situation that they certainly don't want to be in. They may feel taken advantage of and that the Feds targeted them. So after living through it, I was left determined not to conform to the majority in their beliefs. Sure, I felt like a battered spouse beaten into submission, but I couldn't do my time as a bitter person. Being an idealistic guy, I was always trying to prop up the positive instead of dwelling on the negative. It didn't always go over very well, and I realized that guys with idle time in an uncomfortable position simply like to wallow in each other's desolation.

Irritation can come easy in life but often leads to being ashamed of showing this anger. Being humbled and embarrassed by my own annoyances made me start to really ponder what my true worries were: being bothered because of the lack of something. In prison it isn't necessarily rough because of where you are at, but it's troubling because of where you are not. The lack of your presence in the world is lost on the authority figures in these places, but it is certainly prevalent through the conscience of each inmate you talk to every single day.

This absence burdens families. It is this yearning that encumbers society. It is this longing that hurts men and leads to outward ridicule of their current situation. But it is not one's presence inside the prison that is the major struggle. It's knowing that you have no control over what is happening on the outside. You will have no memory of the days and events missed, because you were never there. No matter how many phone calls you make or emails and letters you might send, the years in prison are years that you can never get back. It is sad remembering this reality. Just recalling this really makes me want to bitch.

A brief visit with my family before running off and being busy with life in 2004. From left to right Grams Pat, Kristin, Corbin, Mom Cheryl, Tyler.

Reconciling with my childhood friends helped heal my soul and accept forgiveness. From left to right Brett, Quentin, Corbin, Jon, David.

DIESEL THERAPY

"My scars remind me
that I did indeed survive my deepest wounds."
—Steve Goodier

Anything associated with prison is about punishment. Simply being there establishes the idea of reprimand while your sentence of years behind bars resembles a "time-out" from society. Whatever we did to get there was considered too extreme for normal people to have to deal with, so the judge would give us 5, 10, or 20 years to reflect and fix our rambunctious lifestyles. We were sentenced as punishment to be segregated from the real world and put away on a shelf to pay the price for breaking the laws of the United States.

Then, while serving our punishment, we were always on the brink of being issued more penalties or consequences. For instance, at Leavenworth we were punished as a group—the entire prison population—depending on the situation. The administration was always looking for ways to take things away from us or keep us suppressed further than we already were. The judge and prosecuting attorney saw their opportunity to put us away as a chance to exert their power into our lives. Then many other people along the way during the journey through the federal system took it upon themselves to treat us like crap, whether it be the jailer at the holding facility moving us from intake to our holding pod or the guard who released our unit for lunch each day. Many spoke to us with contempt and looked for something to dishonor us about so we could fix ourselves and get better. It was tiring, and we had to have our wits about us constantly.

While I was at Leavenworth, there were a few key issues that the administration was determined to eradicate from the institution. It was early fall, and the weather was just beginning to find its chill. College football and NFL games were just starting to get underway on the television. It provided something in common for us inmates, an activity we could agree on and look forward to almost every night of the week.

One of the problems that existed recently was the drugs that had been found in the compound. Somehow, a select few inmates were getting illegal drugs into the prison, but the guards kept finding their hiding spots. No single person could be nailed with possession since they were found in common areas not associated with any particular inmate. So the threat came from the authorities that if drugs were found again, then the TVs would be taken away. The masses would be punished for the actions of a few. This type of group punishment was typical in prison because the authorities wanted us to take care of the problem within our own ranks so they didn't have to actually eradicate the problems themselves.

Well, the guys doing the drugs didn't care about the football games on television, and when this contraband was again found a week later, the TVs were indeed removed from the facility. This was a bummer for most of the population, and it didn't eradicate the drug use one bit. We were without televisions for a month, a slow time as I remember. It created a lot of tension between inmates, especially those who tried to take matters into their own hands.

So the drug use led to fights on the compound. It was easy for the guards to see which inmates were involved in the fights since they were the ones who typically broke them up. One particular time, two inmates started yelling at each other near the front offices. It was a racial thing, one white guy disrespecting a black man, saying that he wasn't qualified to work with him out at the golf course. Something about how the black guy didn't belong out there and how he wouldn't be able to control himself around classy women. The black guy didn't take kindly to the remarks and proceeded to slug the old, snobby white-collar convict a few times, bloodying his eye socket and lip.

Both inmates went to the Hole so the situation could be investigated and sorted out. Annoyingly, the entire population of the prison was also locked down for several days. It was as if we were all being punished for the actions of these two disagreeable gentlemen. The administration claimed it was for safety reasons, but it simply seemed like another way for them to exert their power and keep us down. But what could we do? We retreated to our bunks and were stationed there for the next few days until they announced that the Camp was back to a normal schedule.

Another situation did have logic behind it, although it didn't make my stay at Leavenworth any easier. It occurred during my second summer there in 2016. I was taking some drug rehabilitation and counseling classes in the mornings, while working out at the Community Service Garden Project in the afternoons. In the evenings, I would exercise at the weight pile with a group of guys who were also attending the drug counseling classes. It was our way of making good use of our time while trying to find a healthy balance in our lives before we exited prison and were released back into the real world. All these activities were helpful in getting my life back in order.

I noticed over the course of a few months that several of the guys I was working out with were gaining much more weight than I was. They were lifting more and becoming more active in the weight area. They were also spending more private time alone, taking longer showers together, playing cards in the back corner of the library, and eating their meals off to one side of the chow hall. I took note of it but didn't think about their activities too much. It was best to let guys do their time however they wanted, as long as it didn't bother other people.

Then some things started to unfold which made more sense to me. One evening, a stash of drugs was found near one of my buddy's bunks. But it wasn't pot or heroin. Steroids were found along with needles, creatine, amphetamines, and other weight gaining powders—all considered contraband and not allowed on the compound. The administration stated very clearly that if any of these items were found again, then the weights and all the workout equipment would be removed from the facility. It was actually a threat that seemed sensible. Punish the people affected by the problem being presented. The people who cared most about the weights would be the people who were using the steroids.

So the threat was made, and I was sure the problem would subside. Numerous guys used the workout area and most of them didn't want to get that perk taken away from them. I heard inmates constantly talking about getting out of prison and going back home looking rough and tough, like a true felon should. It was the cool thing for some guys to do in prison. To get big, show *off their muscles, and go back home looking hard.*

Unfortunately, about three weeks later there were more steroids found near the same bunk. It didn't take long for the authorities to give the order for the weight pile and workout area to be dismantled. By week's end, it was finished and the exercise area was gone. Now the only workouts available were taking walks around a track and doing push-ups on a concrete slab. Guys tried to collect rocks to lift as weights or use shirts to fashion pull-up bars, but it wasn't the same. I simply resorted to jogging and concentrated on getting more reading in during my free time. I wasn't concerned about getting big anyhow, only being in better shape than I had been in when I showed up.

Within weeks, I noticed my workout buddies getting smaller. Their shoulders weren't as rounded, and their chests didn't seem puffed out anymore. Morale was also down; their once hyper and focused attention was distracted. They all talked about changing their diets to get more "cut up." They concocted excuses about how big muscles weren't healthy, and their new goals were to leave prison lean and ripped, not bulky and beefy. I just let them talk, not commenting one way or another. There was no need to question their motives. People can be whoever they want, and my pals were certainly allowed to change their story anytime they wanted. I went along with it.

To this day there is still one mystery within this scenario that I don't want to solve. I understand why they were using the drugs. Steroids help a person lift more and gain weight in the form of larger muscles. They help boost the ego and give a person energy to overcome shortcomings in other areas of life.

There was, however, one more bottle that turned up with the drugs that the guards had found, and they never really mandated the correct punishment for it. The authorities glossed over the fact that a bottle of Viagra was found with the steroids and other weight-gaining substances. I'm not sure what appropriate punishment could be given in accordance with these ED pills. The one thing that they can't take away from us in prison is our time, because all we have in there is time. But one thing became clear. It now made more sense why my buddies were spending time alone in the showers and keeping private time in the back corners of the library. It turns out that those little blue pills are still popular without women around. A man's needs don't disappear while he is in prison.

###

Being able to bounce back in life is critical to survival, let alone success on this planet. Whether it be in jobs, school, or simply dealing with unforeseen events, the ability to adapt to the flow of life is important. If there is something that will test the resiliency of a person, it is going through transit with the Bureau of Prisons. For each individual, this is a process that can take days, weeks, or months of being moved to different facilities in order to get each prisoner to their next landing spot. It is a trying and uncomfortable situation where the inventory is rendered completely in the hands of the federal marshals. While dealing with my personal adventure, I was acutely aware that this was one of those life situations that I would be better off for having lived through. I had heard other guys talk about it, and so I prepared myself mentally and psychologically when my time finally came to go through transit.

A joke between inmates in the federal prison system is that BOP (Bureau of Prisons) stands for Backwards on Purpose because of how things are run and how people are handled.

It became quite apparent to me during transit that this is the case. We are treated like mushrooms: kept in the dark and fed shit. I'm not sure what other men and women went through, but this is an account of my experience.

My journey started when I was in jail in Kansas City, Missouri, for a few days before being taken an hour and a half outside the city to a small county jail in Osceola, Missouri. This county jail also operates as a federal holding facility for inmates in the region, as do many other county jails across the nation. With the continual increase of the prison population, the Feds had to start farming out where they housed inmates by setting up contracts with jails that wanted to handle the extra work. This was and still is big business for these small towns like Osceola, as it brings federal dollars to these rural communities in the form of added correctional officer jobs and financial support to the sheriff of the county. It was like being in the county pokey, except there were hundreds of us jammed into small holding pods in which we lived for months on end until we were sentenced and shipped off to whatever institution we were assigned to.

I spent about seven months in this place, where we were locked down in our cells (which are about the size of an apartment bathroom) part of the day and let out into a small day room (about the size of an apartment living room) to eat, make phone calls, play cards, and move around a little. There were 13 of us in H Pod in St. Claire County Jail in Osceola, Missouri. The world quickly shrinks, and you are obligated to get used to the new environment.

I had finally been sentenced to 90 months by the time I was used to the routines, the people, and the dynamics of this first spot. Since I had been to court several times, I was often asked by the newer guys what they should expect. It helped me gain their respect, since I helped counsel them on what I had gone through to help prepare them for what they might do to help their current situations. Even though I was getting established in Osceola, I knew in the back of my mind that my current situation could change unexpectedly at any moment. I could be moved to another facility whenever they scheduled a bus transfer.

Just as I was getting used to the place, a guard got my attention right after evening count to tell me that I would be leaving early in the morning before breakfast and shipped to another facility. He didn't tell me where I would be going, only to have myself together when they came back to get me. So that was that. I would soon be on to the next thing, and I would have to start all over at the bottom end of the social hierarchy at whatever new institution they were taking me to.

True to their word, they came pounding on my cell door in the middle of the night and off I went. Looking back, this part of my transit was the most tolerable. I finally got to spend the day in a van with a few other inmates outside of the hole I'd been living in for the past seven months.

It took the better part of a day to go back through Kansas City and stop at a few other jails to pick up and drop off, similar to a bus line or subway. I was shackled at the wrists and at the ankles. There was a chain wrapped around my waist that was attached to my feet and hands to keep my motion and movement to a minimum. It was uncomfortable, but I was hopeful that the next spot would be better. The idea in my mind was that there would be more space to move around and maybe a larger day room. Also, I expected that there would be recreation time in a yard that was outside. I sorely missed the sun and air, since Osceola didn't have outdoor recreation, only the odor of murky concrete walls and grubby painted metal.

That day of transit, less than a year into my sentence, finished at a place called CCA (Corrections Corp of America) in Leavenworth, Kansas. This was a larger holding facility that housed several thousand inmates, all still waiting to be shipped to a more permanent prison where they would serve out the years of their sentence. CCA was an improvement, as the day room was significantly larger and we had the opportunity to go to outdoor recreation a few times a week. I still remember the feeling of spending an hour outside in the rec yard for the first time in months. The brush of the air on my skin was so refreshing that I didn't want to even talk to anyone. That would only ruin the moment of elation that I was feeling. Just smiling and looking up to the sky made me feel like a human again, if only for a moment.

There was me, an inmate named Chris from east KC, and a big guy with bushy red hair and a beard. It was cold out, probably 20 degrees, so nobody else wanted to go to rec that day. But we did. No matter how cold it was, I was experiencing real air again and it was going to be beautiful. The only words I recall as they popped the metal door open with a jolt and a beep were from Chris. In true gangster form he belted out, "Man, I needed this shit right herrre!" I knew he was being sincere even if I wasn't used to all the lingo he and his buddies used in prison. No one uttered a sound for several minutes after that. The understood silence told me that each man was in his own head for a bit collecting memories and gaining steam with our current reality.

The prison guard monitoring us broke the silence. "You guys! Rec is for 20 minutes today! That door stays locked until I say so. You can walk around on the concrete, but stay away from the fences." Nobody else said anything, so I responded with, "Yes sir!" That's all I usually said to the guards. They didn't want any more than that out of me, and I certainly didn't want to stand out. Just a guy wearing orange that was of no threat to them—that's all I wanted to be right now in their eyes.

The moment went swiftly, as all good moments do. About a dozen laps around the concrete, slow and plodding. Several things were important to me during those 20 minutes. I took deep meaningful breaths, inhaling energy from my higher power. There was soft, blissful prayer giving thanks for the moment. Then finally, engaging in gentle conversation with the other two inmates out there with me. We walked past pull-up bars, a basketball goal, a few metal benches, and a wall used for handball. But we weren't interested in any of that. Just the slow shuffle of feet, our hands inside our issued jackets. It was as peaceful of a moment that I had experienced up to that point. I'm glad that the three of us were on the same page for our 20-minute stroll.

I stayed at CCA for about seven weeks, and I knew it would only be a temporary abode. It was a very transient facility as there were people coming and going every day. Some guys had been there for the better part of a year and some even longer, but the majority of us were just passing through like ships in the night. I minded my own time at this place and waited until the day that one of the officers would come bearing the same news that I was to get myself together and leave this holding facility as well.

From observing how other inmates had been informed of their departures, I understood that I would not be given much notice. I also knew, after being moved a few times now, that I would be stripped out, poked, prodded, and checked before leaving this place for my next destination. The intake and discharge in these facilities are some of the more annoying times where you wait like cattle locked up in a series of cold holding cells. Everything you have accumulated up to that point is taken away and a new set of pajama-like clothes are issued to you. This prevents an inmate from taking items from one place to the next. If you had important items like court papers or medicine, then they were mailed separately and would meet you at your next destination.

Other than getting outside for the first time in seven months, my stay was calm at CCA. I spent my time reading, eating, and doing push-ups. I conversed with only a few people here and there, but with the constant influx and outflow of inmates, it was difficult to establish any friendships. Simply waiting my turn to go was my focus.

After several weeks of keeping to myself, I was again given the news that I would be leaving soon and to have myself ready when they returned. In less than an hour the COs were back, so I left my extra white shirt and a few packages of tuna with my cellmates while sharing my farewells. I was looking forward to this move with the hope that again it would be a little better than this spot. I also welcomed the travel on the bus. The last day of travel only a handful of weeks earlier was bearable, and the scenery brought about a welcome change in my attitude. I looked forward to being in a place other than the cell I had been stuck in, cramped and smelling of other men.

But this bus ride didn't turn out as pleasant as I foolishly predicted. It was one of the most dreadful 14 hours I could have imagined spending in overnight transit. In leaving, they stripped us down naked, gave us toilet paper thin pants and shirts to wear, again shackled our wrists and ankles, and attached the around-the-waist chain to restrict our movements. Two things were different this time. Two things that made sitting on a rigid seat locked in a prison bus one of the crappiest overnights I've lived through.

First, they used the dreaded black box to restrict the movement of our hands even more than they already were. This black box positions your wrists about a foot apart from each other and keeps you from being able to scratch an itch, fix your clothes that were continually falling down, or rest both of your arms at the same time. In other words, some parts of your upper limbs were always flexed to keep the other parts of your body at rest. Because of being bound like this, we were deterred from messing with the other prisoners. This practice also kept the transit uneventful for the officers transporting us. It was like doing some sort of core workout or plyometric exercise for 14 hours straight. Agonizing and tiresome.

The second thing that made this trip a hard memory to shake is that I was physically chained to the guy next to me. I'm sure many of you have seen this before in movies or TV, but this was different. We were chained at the waist as to be like Siamese twins or something. The only wisdom I gained from this is that now I have a feeling of what Matt Damon and Greg Kinnear went through while filming the movie *Stuck on You*.

Trying to balance the black box and waist attachment along with the standard wrist and ankle restraints took a mental toll on me quickly. To get through it, I tapped into some advice from my uncle who is a retired Navy SEAL. He is a tough-as-nails human being who inspires me every time I'm able to spend time with him. I recalled some training stories he had passed on to me about things he and his comrades would do to prepare for the extreme situations they might find themselves in while in the field. I thought of the exercises he had told me about and the cold, wet conditions he had trained in to prepare his body for whatever the world would throw at him. He taught me when I was young that the mind is the key to any tough situation. His mantra was always to keep the mind right and your body and wit will follow. I kept my brain in check and maintained my mental toughness throughout the bus ride. Often, I would quiet my mind, concentrate on a loved one that I missed so much, or prepare myself for arriving at a new prison, which is usually a circus for the first 24 hours.

Meditation, prayer, and sheer will got me through that night. Dozens of times I would be shaken back into reality by a hard bump or the loud complaints of another inmate. It was within an hour of the start of the bus trip that we were all extremely worn out. The bus ride was either dead quiet or heavy with the chatter of sharp objections. Many of the men were full of anger and angst. It was difficult to quiet the mind, but I used this moment in my life as a refining exercise—motivated by the stories I had stored away in my memory told to me by my Uncle Tim.

Yes, it was grueling. I do not share the mental acuteness and strength of the greatest warriors in the world. I did, however, use the Navy SEALs as motivation that night. Moreover, I leaned greatly on the transcendent power of keeping the mind still through meditation, focusing on God and His energy within me to continue. It was this overnight event that shored up my confidence in the power of prayer and the blessings that come from true faith.

The moment they chained us together and marched us on the bus, I knew this ride would take its toll on me. Immediately, I got in the mindset that I wouldn't let the bus beat me. I purposely picked out a few guys sitting near me that I could talk with positively. I drew certain jokes or stories from my memory that would keep us uplifted. In times of silence, I would focus on light, pure energy refueling me. We weren't allowed to move around, but my mind was flush with vigor.

The men on this bus were not happy, and morale was low. When I wasn't meditating, I mentioned sports and even tried to get guys to argue over NFL teams. Quarreling over football was at least better than spiraling down into pity over our back soreness. I attempted to get guys to open up about their backgrounds, and that worked too. People love to tell another human how their lives have unfolded and especially how they ended up in federal prison. My attempts didn't work every time, but I'm sure they helped. It helped me anyhow.

Other times I would sit in silence and focus on building a house from the ground up. Pouring the foundation, putting up the studs, hoisting the trusses, and designing how the rooms would be mapped out. So many things go into constructing a home, so I was able to submerse my mind into this activity for good chunks of time. I even got to the point where I was picking out the wood finishes for the cabinets in the kitchen. The house was never completed, but it was always a task I could go back to and draw time from. Time away from my tense head and confused torso.

As the sun sprung over the horizon, highway signs read that we were in Arkansas nearing Little Rock. This meant that our destination would be Forrest City, Arkansas, which is near Memphis, Tennessee. There's a large FCC facility there, and this is where I was about to spend the next part of my sentence. Knowing my next landing spot didn't make the ride any easier; it only proved to me the finality of my bus trip. That this too, like all things in life, shall pass. Watching the miles click down on these road signs gave me hope, however slow they unfolded. But hope is a pleasant thing when you can keep it out in front of you and steady the mind. In this case, it helped me to pull through the current anguish and kept time moving forward.

Arriving at the Forrest City Prison we drove into the 15,000-acre facility toward the first large complex of buildings. In the distance we could see that they were surrounded by a large system of razor-wire fencing. Imposing, yet expected with the experience I had gained over the past nine months of incarceration. I happened to glance to my left and noticed a smaller building without a fence that looked like a dormitory. Out front there was a sign that read Camp—I had heard of these before. This was the minimum-security building designated for minor, nonviolent offenders and people with short sentences, mostly white-collar guys or drug dealers that worked their way down over the years from a higher-security facility. I viewed it as a reward for good behavior. If one has to do some years in a federal prison, the Camp is the place to be, in my opinion. Not so oppressive or anxiety riddled for a guy like me who isn't necessarily cut out for the rough life inside the walls. I saw the building and started to hope that my stop would be there, and my time might start to be a little easier than it had begun.

Just then, a guard from the front of the bus shouted that nobody would be going to the Camp today and that we shouldn't get our hopes up. It was certainly depressing how quickly any buildup of positivity can be dashed by the people who were in charge of us in this system. It's as if they were put there or chose to work in this profession strictly to inflict discomfort and worry onto those under their watch.

So instead, I started to prepare myself for being assigned to either the FCI (which is a medium-security facility and full of gangs and crews) or the FCC (which is considered the low-security facility, but still with thousands of inmates and trouble looming around every corner). I would have to find "my people" immediately upon entering and make sure they approved of me, my charges, and my worth to whatever activities they were involved with in that particular prison. Yes, things were about to get more real even after this nightmarish 14-hour bus ride of soreness.

We passed the Camp and headed toward the FCI. While pulling into the front next to a sally port (a double-door-lock sort of entrance) with an electronically operated gate, the guard started calling out names of inmates. These individuals were to prepare to exit the bus. This really just meant to remain seated and to not move until the guards came and unchained us from each other. But from the announcement, I sensed the tension start to rise. My name was not called, but about 12 others were. These guys now knew that the next many years of their life would be spent behind the gates they were about to walk through. I watched as two trucks pulled up outside the bus and men with shotguns positioned themselves, locked and loaded, with barrels pointed to where the prisoners were about to line up. It is a bit unnerving to have a shotgun pointed at you in any situation. You never know what the guy in front of you is going to do; it's just such an unpredictable existence moment-to-moment.

I sighed a quiet relief as the guys assigned to the FCI began to disembark from the bus and march themselves inside prison. The tension was ratcheted up for them, but it began to dissipate for us. Looking around, I observed the 20 or so guys left in the bus and now realized that they would be assigned with me at the FCC. We wouldn't be going to the Camp, but this facility lowered our chances of violence upon arrival, at least that is what I had convinced myself.

It didn't take long for them to empty the first 12 inmates, and we were on our way down the road to another large concrete building surrounded by razor wire. It looked similar to the prison where we had just deposited the other guys except for the sign out front that read "Forrest City Federal Correctional Complex, Administrative Low Facility." We offloaded here and began our intake. It was a relief to get out of the bus and improve the circulation in my arms and legs. This process was not to be quick, though, and we spent every bit of another four-hour stretch getting processed into our new "home." Waiting mostly, a lot of waiting with fits and bursts of pictures, medical questions, and a sack lunch with a bologna sandwich and a stale cookie. It's known among those who have done any sort of time that the foremost activity in prison is waiting.

After all the initial steps of getting received into FCC Forrest City, I was given a bundle with clothes, blankets, and a sheet. Hurriedly, a short but stern woman yelled at me to report to Cell House HD. A door opened, and she communicated through walkie-talkie that an inmate would be walking through. I was led onto a large empty yard with sidewalks snaking toward each building. It was the embodiment of institutional living, with grey concrete buildings, no trees, grey skies, and an eerie feeling of despair in the air.

I felt nervous as hell knowing that this was only year one of a seven-and-a-half-year sentence. This had been the longest nine months of my life so far, and I had so much of my sentence left to do. How was I expected to keep my mind straight in this place? It was a relief to be at a spot knowing that I wasn't locked in a small room most of the day, but this was the real show now. The moment had arrived to dig into my time like a champ—there was no other way around it.

A man is only as solid as his word and character in this place because he has nothing else to hang his hat on. No cushy job to boast of in front of new acquaintances. No home to run back to if the day became overwhelming. No family to surround yourself with and help reassure you on a sad day. No old friends to turn to for advice when confronted with unusual circumstances. Not even a familiar road to drive and ponder to collect your thoughts after a full day. Only the traits you were born with and the direction of your higher power. If you were smart, then this was the time where you prayed that a higher power was watching and guiding you.

It took a laborious three minutes as I sauntered across the empty yard to the HD dorm. All these concerns and many more fleeting thoughts blazed through my mind as I prepared to enter into this next chapter of my life. It was to be a defining time in my journey, and I made sure I ingested every moment of every event. I completed my walk up a set of stairs to stand outside the metal door and paused for the guard on the other end to unlock it and order me through.

Standing outside the building, I wondered why it was so quiet. I could hear the wind blowing—it was warm for a late February afternoon. It was odd to think that there were about two thousand men in this facility and I couldn't hear a single one of them at this moment. Was this common here? Did something happen that kept the guys subdued into submission? Then with a jolt, the metal door opened from inside and a correctional officer barked at me to get in. He scolded that there was a move coming up and I was in the way standing by the door. I didn't know what a "move" was, but I assumed it had to do with how the prison relocated inmates around the facility. The place was quite expansive, and the sidewalks leading to other buildings obviously were used for something.

I soon learned that at the top of every hour during the day there was a 10-minute span of time where inmates could move about the compound to wherever they needed to be. The library, rec yard, education building, medical unit, etc., were all places we were allowed to be, and once you got there during this move, you had to stay at that location until the next move. It was a simple way of controlling inmate traffic around the compound to keep the place safe and organized.

The activity we now called "move" was about to become an important part of a daily routine in my new existence. People were always planning around the next move—waiting so they could go exercise, head to the library for some reading materials, or make their way to a work assignment. Often inmates would ask each other if a move had started or if the move had ended yet, wondering if there was still time to change locations. Getting used to a life based on when you can move is a big part of becoming institutionalized.

So entering the unit, I was immediately shocked by the rowdy noise. It was in sharp contrast to the peace and quiet outside. I was a new fish standing there with my bundle and stupid-looking face, not knowing what to do next. Then a voice came on the overhead speakers announcing that the compound was open for a 10-minute move, and the whole place became busy. The song *Ants Marching*, by Dave Mathews, ran through my brain as I tried to grasp how and why everyone was suddenly so busy. I also realized that it really had nothing to do with me right now, and so I looked for where the cells were and who my bunkie would be.

Just then a husky white guy in good athletic shape with a twang in his voice that reminded me of Oklahoma or North Texas approached me, asking where I was from and what I was looking for. I quickly realized that he was a shot-caller of some sort and possibly the head of the car that I would be riding with while at this place. The term "car" referred to those people that you ran around with, participated in activities with, such as working out and eating, and generally who you spent your time with. I was aware of how things worked and understood that I needed to be on good working terms with him if things were to go well for me here. Each of us newbies became associated with a group of people, usually those who were from the same part of the country as ourselves. I suspected this was my guy since he already seemed to know a little about me.

He introduced himself as Ronnie and asked what I wanted to be called. Interesting that he didn't ask my name, only what he should call me. I didn't know it at the time, but in prison guys often take on a nickname to stay somewhat anonymous. We would all spend years together in this place but were not necessarily friends. This was also seen as one of those cool things that you could do in prison, change your identity and be whatever you could live up to in this new environment. Ronnie seemed serious and insisted that he would now walk me around the unit and clue me in to how things were run in there. So I quickly began to pay attention to what was said and shown to me.

First impressions mean a lot in prison, as they do in the real world, so I showed respect, listened intently, and followed him as he began to show me around the unit. It was a whirlwind, and

I did the best I could to keep my composure while attempting to decipher all this new information at once. Who was who in the hierarchy of prisoners here? Where was I allowed to hang out and where was my bunk? What did I need to do to get adjusted and best help my social standing in my new situation? I did the best I could to keep it together. For better or worse, things were off and running for me at the Forrest City low-security facility.

Of all the events that took place on that day, I knew I wanted to take one thing very seriously, so I took immediate steps to enact my intentions. I talked to Ronnie, my new shot-caller, about how I would get a seat in the white-guy TV room (segregation is prominent in prison). I knew by now that in prison a good amount of time can be spent by watching TV together with a group of guys that you got along with. It was a form of bonding and support, and it eased the stress of our tense existence in this place. Ronnie took me to the white-guy TV room, introduced me to the guys in there at the time, and acknowledged that I would be screened to see if I could be an addition to the room when the time was right. You see, things were not always straightforward in prison, and the other guys had to make sure you were a solid enough dude to be in there with them. It was their reputation that was on the line, depending on who they hung out with.

After we left the TV-room group, Ronnie took me aside and informed me of the steps that had to be taken for me to get in with them. First, he had to ask around to see if anyone else knew me from the streets to make sure I wasn't a flake. Next, he would watch me around the compound for a few weeks to see how I carried myself and make sure I wasn't some lame ass, bonehead, or troublemaker. Finally, he wanted to see my paperwork to make sure I wasn't a snitch, child molester, rapist, or other kind of sexual predator. Even though we were all in prison, some charges were deemed more desirable than others. Fortunately, I had paperwork proving that I had drug distribution charges, which put me on the good side of what crimes to commit (according to inmates that is), and my papers indicated that I had not snitched on anyone or committed any sexual misconduct or child molestation offenses. I quickly got on Ronnie's good side, and my status rapidly ascended at Forrest City, FCC.

Things progressed as well as they could. My life as a federal inmate took form in this new social system in which I was learning to live. Ronnie put in a good word for me, and I got a job in the paint shop over in the facilities department. I met a guy that we called T.T. (which stood for Too Tall since he was about six foot eight) who was from Columbia, Missouri. He and I got along, and I felt we were cut from the same cloth. He showed me the ropes and got me accustomed to how things operated in this place. As social as he was, it helped me to meet the other inmates. Conveniently, he lived in my unit and we spent a lot of evenings watching TV together. I recall regularly watching *The Voice* and whatever was showing on AMC.

T.T. introduced me to guy called Bleach (not his real name), who was from Chicago. Bleach became my next bunkmate and also helped the transition into my new surroundings. He and I could not have been any more different. He sported tattoos from head to toe in all shapes and colors, while I resembled the average white dude who could have been in prison for tax evasion or mail fraud. Nonetheless, Bleach and I had some good talks over my first several months, and he helped me get a grip on how to bear down and do my time wisely. One thing he said to me will stay with me forever. He said, "CB, man ... you have to do the time ... you can't let the time do you." I thought about what he said, and I realized that I couldn't avoid being in prison. I was here regardless of what I wanted, and I had to accept the fact that I would be in this system for years to come. The best thing to do was to just let the wave of my situation wash over me and be in the present. This really is true in all areas of life, not just for the unfortunate souls that go to prison.

As the months passed, I couldn't get the memory of seeing the minimum-security Camp out of my head. Things were going fine, but it was still prison. When a person is confined behind walls and razor wire, he yearns for something more. Mental weariness is an invading feeling, and I was already starting to sense it even in my short stint. After a few months in, I asked my case manager what, if anything, I needed to do to get to a Camp and make my time a little easier. She looked at my file on her computer for a few minutes, asked me some questions, and then looked at me square in the face. She stated in a very matter of fact tone that I actually wasn't far off from being Camp eligible. She suggested a few programming classes to take and reminded me to stay out of trouble. In six months I was to report back to her and see about my status then.

I left her office with a bounce in my step and a new mission for my immediate future. I am a person who likes to see things through to success, so this was an exciting goal for me to strive toward. In my mind I knew that there was a Camp at the Leavenworth Prison, and if this plan could get me there, then I would be close to home in a facility that would allow me a better work assignment. It would also afford me the opportunity to be around guys who were from my area of the country. All things moving me in the right direction so I could get my life back on track.

The next six months went as planned, and when I walked into my case manager's office, I was armed with answers and prayers. She reviewed my progress, asked me some simple questions, and then asked me to leave her office. I was somewhat concerned at this request, but she then told me to check back in 20 minutes. The following 20 minutes were spent in deep, meaningful prayer and meditation. I wanted, more than anything at that point in my life, to get assigned to the Camp at Leavenworth. I also wanted, more than anything, to accept whatever it was that God had planned for me in this moment of my life.

I sat in my cell focused on the light from above shining down on me and endowing me with a calm of presence and peace in my heart. God wants each of us to be happy and fulfilled in life, and I hoped that my feelings and his plans were one and the same. This was one of the numerous times that there were tears in my eyes during the six years I spent in prison, and they were tears of appreciation that I was content with whatever was about to happen to me in this moment.

Well, 20 minutes actually goes by quite quickly when you reach a true meditative state, so with prepared focus, I marched back to her office to see what my updated status was that day. I opened the door and sat down quietly in front of her desk. She looked up at me and asked with a still and stoic tone, "... which Camp facility you would like to request for your transfer?" Immediately I understood and struggled to contain my excitement. It was a strain to answer her because she said I needed to give her my top three choices. I blurted out Leavenworth and whatever the next two closest facilities were.

So now it was all happening again. I had already been to four different institutions during my year of incarceration, and I was about to dive into transit again. She informed me that it would take a few months for the paperwork to go through, so now it was just a waiting game. Then it dawned on me. More travel on that bus that brought me here would absolutely suck. The last transfer took around 14 hours to get from Kansas City to Forrest City, so I assumed it would be another trip similar to the first. If I needed to wrap my mind around that situation, I could do it. I convinced myself that I could do anything as long as I could get my mind in the right place for this next adventure. The following months went by smoothly, and I got the impression I would be getting my transfer after the first of the year.

Sure enough, the second week of January, I was awoken at about 4:30 a.m. and told to get myself together and to meet up at the front door of the unit in 20 minutes. It was here, my day to get transferred to a Camp and the day things would start getting even better for me.

As expected, it took several hours to get discharged from the facility. Once again, it felt novel to be on the road and doing something different. We were all in an uncomfortable prison bus shackled at wrists, feet, and around the waist again. I noticed the bus was headed toward Memphis, but I wasn't too concerned. I was on my way to a Camp. These other guys in the bus, which numbered about 20, must be going somewhere, too, and maybe we had several stops to make.

When we went through Memphis and arrived at the prison, I wasn't too worried. We picked up some more prisoners and then hit the road again. It was arriving at the airport in Memphis that got me a little suspicious. You see, while in transit, the guards don't give you any info as to where the bus is headed, how long it will take, or in general, what the heck is really going on. Remember, mushrooms. Kept in the dark and fed shit. So we got to the airport and pulled to a corner of the tarmac. There we waited for an airplane, another bus, or more people. I still wasn't quite sure.

We had been sitting for about an hour when a nondescript plane with no markings pulled up. Federal marshals deployed the aircraft and took positions at strategic locations around the plane and buses. They began to methodically take prisoners off the plane one by one. More buses began to pull up, and different guys were put on various transports and taken away. There were lots of federal marshals and even more prisoners. The plane was full of over a hundred men and women in custody, while at least 50 more waited to be shuffled onto the plane at some point. This was my first experience of what the Feds call Con Air. It was not necessarily as intimidating as is portrayed in movies, but the officers and administrators are certainly serious and meticulously organized.

It was apparent that there were inmates from all over the place. Some didn't speak English, others were dressed in street clothes, while some looked as if they had been locked in a cell for a decade or more. I didn't feel threatened by any of the inmates, but when a federal marshal points a shotgun at you in the direction he wants you to walk, it is a little intimidating. If this is how American citizens are treated, then I wonder what it's like for accused terrorists or prisoners of war. Keeping order is important, but it's very unlikely that guys who are in thin sandals, T-shirts, pajama pants, and shackled at the wrists and ankles have a fighting chance to make an escape. Nonetheless, we were herded onto the plane and told to keep the conversation to a minimum. I thought to myself that a plane ride would at least make things a little more interesting, while in turn the trip to the KC area would only take about an hour or so. Much improved over that stern bus ride I was anticipating.

The plane ride was quiet; I mostly stared straight ahead and tried to keep my mind at ease. After about an hour, we began our descent and I looked out the window expecting to recognize the familiar surroundings of the Kansas City area. Green fields, beautiful suburban subdivisions, and maybe even a distinguishing glimpse of the historic downtown area. The first things I noticed, however, were the fir trees and orange soil. We hadn't flown far, but where could we be? Nashville? Oklahoma City? It wasn't my beloved Kansas City for sure, and this trip had just taken a turn for the unknown. I heard a guy near me mention that it was possibly Atlanta, which seemed logical. The time frame made sense at least.

I looked out the window and recognized some of the larger buildings that paint the skyline of downtown Atlanta. Considering my new location left me frustrated, and I dwelled on how this stop had taken me further from my desired destination. By then, anxiety began to build up inside me.

This is where a unique hour of my life took place and when one of the most memorable of my transit memories occurred. After being told to depart the plane, I made my way down the stairs and one of the marshals ordered me to board the bus over to the right. I looked over and couldn't help but notice painted on the side of the bus in large letters was USP Atlanta. USP stands for United States Penitentiary, which indicated that it was a maximum-security facility. USP Atlanta was one of the first federal prisons built in the US and still is notorious for housing some of the roughest of the rough. Gang leaders, lifetime criminals, guys that were sequestered away from society for safety reasons. I wasn't too excited about this next part of my journey, but I waddled my way toward my new ride in an orderly fashion.

A few sparks from my memory joined me on my march toward the USP bus. Recollections of my carefree youth at summer camps in the Flint Hills of central Kansas. Swimming in warm lakes, hiking through cottonwood-filled forests, fishing for catfish and jumping across creeks with close friends. Those young years taught me to be resourceful, respectful, and reliable—lessons that I would take with me through life. I tried to dig deep now for those qualities and rely on them in a more survival-necessary situation. I considered what those friends of mine from my early years would think of me now? It had been so long since those joyous summers that they were now pushed into the recesses of our memories, much to be forgotten.

Shaken back into reality now, a line of us approached the USP Atlanta bus and I heard gangster rap blaring through the door we were about to enter. The correctional officer driving the bus was a serious dark-skinned guy with his black hat on backward and aviator sunglasses squaring out his face. He aimed his gaze toward us and indicated that we should find a seat so we could be on our way. The music escorted us into the bus, and I watched as heavy hitters, tattooed longhairs, and loud Hispanic guys filed in and found their places around me. I immediately took a seat near the front. This surely isn't what I imagined when I was to be transferred. I felt more inadequate at this moment than I had felt in my entire life. This bus ride was shaping up to be an immediate brawl rather than a lengthy insufferable romp like the bus ride I had endured just eight months before.

Finally, a large Islander with bushy hair sat next to me and settled in while the whole seat bank around us shook. He was large enough to command his own seat, so I squished myself up next to the window and decided to sustain another uncomfortable ride. The bus was already loud with the music and now with the jibber-jabber of everyone blowing off steam from the subdued flight. My seat mate didn't say a word to me, and I obliged. This was no time to stand out, so I did my best to assimilate.

The ride took about 20 minutes through some city streets after a brief stint on the freeway. This is when we began to approach an older, more rundown neighborhood. One of the inmates indicated we were getting close to the "ATL USP" as he called it. This guy specified that he had been down at this facility in the '90s for several years.

The neighborhood reeked of destitute, and it seemed as if the negativity of the prison had seeped out into the surrounding streets to decay the soul of the community. This had left the adjacent buildings mere shells of their former selves. It was as depraved as any neighborhood I had ever been through—certainly enough to keep my eyes peeled for interesting characters or even possible crimes in progress.

Pulling up to a stop light, I turned to my left and saw what was either a pimp or drug dealer skipping toward the bus flashing some sort of gang sign. His hand was in the shape a C and held closely to his chest while yelling something about the Crips. All the guys on the bus got riled up and began yelling back. Mind you, there were tinted windows and bars separating us from the outside, but nonetheless they yelled back and forth like they were on the street together. Then, from behind the guy flashing signs on the street came what could only have been a prostitute, judging by the way she was dressed. Short leopard print jacket, high heels, shanty-ripped hose, and boobs hanging out with frizzy hair and makeup for days. She was holding in her hand a mostly empty 40-ounce beer bottle. The next thing she did was throw it toward the bus, shattering it all over the side and getting everyone more excited and louder. I was shocked, entertained, and certainly impressed by the boldness of these local Atlantans. This day had certainly left an impression on me from the minute the shotguns were pointed at my face. I should have been more stunned, but today I wasn't.

What did surprise me is that the guards on the bus didn't seem too startled by the incident. The light turned green, they shouted at the prisoners on the bus to quiet down, and the bus continued on its way. It was as if this was all part of the show on this little amusement ride from hell. A few more blocks and we made our way up to the rugged prison. It was all old concrete, limestone, and brick, and I got the sense that there was a hissing radiator around every corner. It was finished in 1902 and looked to be in general disrepair, just nice enough to house federal inmates.

The intake at this stop again took hours and we ended up being assigned to the transfer portion of the facility. It resembled a dungeon, as it was behind so many locked doors that I lost count. They threw me in a cell with another guy and yelled out "twenty-three and one" while slamming the door behind me. This meant that we were to be locked down in this cell for 23 hours of the day and let out into the day room for one hour each day to make phone calls, shower, and find a book to help pass the time. Again, there was no indication as to how long I would be there, where the transit would head to next, or in general, why the heck I was in Atlanta in the first place.

I looked at the guy who was already in the cell before I got there and asked him what was up with this place. He told me it was a small transfer center in the South and that people were in and out of there all the time. We would be locked down most of the day, so it was smart for us to get used to each other really quick. He told me he was waiting to be transferred and stated that he'd been waiting for about 18 months in that small cell. My heart sank and my head began to hurt. I had heard about transit nightmares where guys got lost in the system and were just shuffled from place to place for years on end before they ended up at the appropriate spot. Like a piece of mail stuck inside a letter carrier's bag. I hoped for the best, but this whole day was not turning out very well at this point. I had been gone from Forrest City for less than 24 hours and felt more lost than ever. Looking back, I actually had a decent thing going at my last spot with the job in the paint shop, being friendly with a few guys, and generally doing my time without worry or trouble. Now, I had taken Con Air to Atlanta, driven through the hood to an old decaying prison, and at last been ordered to a small cell in the basement. This was about as far away from a Camp as I could imagine. Days such as this are a reminder that dinner isn't always better at your neighbor's house. But boy, what I wouldn't have done to be able to see some grass right then, something resembling nature—not just the grey labyrinth that I was currently immersed in. Living among cement and steel was beginning to wear on my well-being, and I yearned again to have the wind blowing against my face and to see trees, shrubs, and rushing rivers.

I ended up staying at the ATL USP for less than 48 hours, but I couldn't help that my anxiety meter was going bonkers. Around what seemed like noon, I was once again asked to gather myself up and off I went through discharge and to the airport.

117

I was being swept away to another facility, and it only made sense that I would be flying into Kansas City this time. Looking back, I had only been gone from Forrest City a few days, and I had already gone through Memphis and ended up in Atlanta. Before my stay at Forrest City, I had been through the CCA in Leavenworth, St. Claire County Federal Holding Facility, and the Downtown Kansas City Jail. I suppose I can count the courthouse holding facility also since I had spent a total of about 30 hours waiting in a holding cell there. I was used to being shuttled around at this point, but I was certainly ready to find a landing spot to spend the next five years of my time. I was praying that Leavenworth would be that place soon enough.

As I again piled onto the plane in organized fashion, I plopped down next to a chatty fellow from Louisiana. We weren't really supposed to talk a whole lot, but he didn't seem to care. I felt like Forest Gump sitting next to Bubba, listening to story after story of what he was involved in before getting caught up in the system. He was a bank robber who also worked on fishing boats and liked to date married women. I really didn't care if his stories were true or not because they were entertaining nonetheless, and his enthusiasm made the hours on the plane go by smoothly. He told me about other prisons he had been at, and it seemed like he didn't mind doing time at the higher-security facilities. I mentioned to him that I hoped we were going to be landing next in Kansas City because I was from around there and wanted to do my time at Leavenworth. He seemed to think that we were headed to the Oklahoma City Transfer Center. Unfortunately this made sense, and I once again began to prepare myself to be housed in another holdover.

By this time, I was used to the procedures. Go through intake and stay calm. Get to my assigned unit and find a cell. Get to know my cellmate and then look around the rest of the unit for my people. I always kept an eye out for those who are like me—race, beliefs, from my part of the country, etc. It just made things easier. Then settle in and don't make waves with the other inmates. If I would conquer those steps successfully, then I knew that I'd be off to a good start. So I decided to get in the right frame of mind and prepare for Oklahoma City.

Sure enough, we landed at the airport and the plane pulled right up to a gate that was attached to a large holding facility. I was not in Kansas City; I was at the Oklahoma City Federal Transfer Center, or OKC, and would have to shore up my faculties for another go around. This place was strange in its own right, and I was just practicing my patience while keeping my wits about me.

OKC turned out to be a peculiar place—it was very transient. People were in and out of the 150-person unit all day and night. It was a busy place, so I was hopeful that I wouldn't be there long enough to care. It's a lockdown facility where the inmates are let out for meals and to make phone calls, emails, shower, or search for a book to occupy their downtime. Other than that, we were locked in our cells all night and a good portion of the day. I wasn't lucky enough for my stay to be short and spent seven weeks at the transfer center before finally catching a bus out late one evening.

My stay was not uneventful, and a few brief memories will remain in my brain kingdom forever. If you can imagine the handful of stereotypical prison scenarios that one might see in a movie, they happened during my stay at Oklahoma City. Once again, we were all being held in a place where there was not much to do other than conjure up a book and wait until the next meal was served. This being the case, everyone was up in each other's business and the tension could escalate without warning.

The first thing I noticed was the number of guys that walked around with a chip on their shoulder. While I was moving down in the custody rankings from a low-security facility to a minimum-security Camp facility, many guys were moving up from a medium to a USP max for violent behavior or investigations that got them more time added to their sentences. They weren't trying to move their way out of the system like I was. No, they were rolling hard and playing the prison game as if it were a way of life—and for them it was. I was on different time than these guys were, and this made it difficult to keep to myself. I tried to mostly stay in my cell and read. But it was more of the same, just waiting until I got the call to get moved on to the next place. The hope was that the next place would be the Camp.

So I tried to stay out of the way, but to no avail. For example, in my second week I was summoned to chat with a guy who was a bank robber from Boston. He had been some kind of shot-caller at his previous spot and was continuing this practice while here at OKC. There were not a whole lot of white guys in our holding pod, so he expressed to me that we had to stick together and everything would stay cool. Additionally, he informed me that a new batch of guys had just shown up and a kid with child molestation charges was among them. He indicated that it was my job to go check him in to prove my worth to our crew. This meant that I was to force him to request protective custody and remove himself from our unit.

This was a shock to me since I wasn't aware that I was part of some crew, and I certainly didn't want to get involved in shaking down another inmate. I only wanted to safely get to the Camp that I had been assigned to. Reasoning with him was not getting me anywhere, and the tension in the room was starting to make my hands sweat and my head hurt.

Well, this was a situation that required my immediate action, so I decided to approach this new young guy whom they had deemed unworthy. It was an unfortunate label that placed him at the bottom of the hierarchy in this place. I was not enjoying my task, but I made sure the situation would be handled in a reasonable manner to keep me from getting into an argument or fight. A fight would ruin my chances of getting to the Camp. I went up to this youngster and basically told him, "Look, I don't care why you are here or what your charges are, but those guys over there do. I was sent over here to tell you to check yourself into the SHU or they'll do it for you."

At about that time, this poor kid got a look of disbelief on his face and told me he had just spent the last 18 months in the SHU. He had not spoken to anyone else in a while, and this was his first taste of being out of his cell and mingling amongst the general inmate population. The SHU is the Special Housing Unit, sometimes called the Hole, the Bucket, or the Cooler back in the day. An inmate put there is kept in a small isolation cell 24/7 usually for reasons of punishment, investigation, transfer, or for personal protection. In his case, he was kept there because if he were allowed to walk out on the yard he would get beat up, picked on, punished, and possibly killed in the right situation. So it was for his safety and also to keep order in the institution. Hearing me say that he needed to check back into the SHU was devastating news.

Now, I felt for the kid. I am 100 percent against what he did out in the world to be put in prison. Anything that has to do with endangering the innocence of a child is despicable and shameful. But as part of my personal rehab and affiliation with God, I gave up my judgement of others' lives. Let's leave that to the source of all energy in the universe. I don't have to agree with what others decide to do, and I still have my opinions and feelings. As a general rule for myself, though, I decided that I am not going to get involved in other people's lives unless it starts to encroach into my life or the lives of those people I love. This situation had bled into my life and so I did the best I could to keep a level head and get the problem solved quickly. It didn't seem like a big deal to the other guys who ran with the shot-caller, but it was nerve-wracking as hell for me. Fortunately, the kid quickly recognized that he should check himself back into the SHU, assuring that peace was kept in the pod for another afternoon.

I still talked to the other white guys in the pod, but over the next few weeks people started getting transferred and the dynamics changed. I spent my afternoons doing pull-ups and reading a stash of sci-fi novels I ran across. I remember this several-week stretch because it helped me understand more deeply what motivates people in a prison setting. I was starting to get better at navigating the daily interactions that make up prison life. It was these small and seemingly insignificant interactions that actually make or break the amount of respect you get in the system, and in turn how easy or difficult your time will be. Every conversation, each shared bit of knowledge, and the favor given or not given is kept track of by someone, because inmates and guards are always watching. From then on, I kept my ears open, my eyes forward, and my conversations strictly focused on what was in it for me. It was my survival technique.

I didn't simply keep to myself though. Interacting with other guys in the pod and initiating some conversation with genuine questions kept my wit sharp. The most interesting talks were with guys I had little in common with or whom I would not normally reach out to in a real-world setting. Notable were several Muslim gentlemen who were nice, friendly, and open to talking about their beliefs. I found more similarities than differences between us, which gave me a fresh perspective about the state of religion in our country. We read all the time in social media posts about choosing love over hate and the importance of accepting others who seem different than ourselves. Here in prison, it was motivating to learn firsthand what that actually feels like. Getting to know someone else wasn't forced, it happened organically since we were all living through the same struggles at that time in our lives.

Another situation that I had to live through in OKC was how I dealt with being propositioned by other men. It wasn't like being hit on by another guy in the world. No, it was more like being harassed by a pushy salesman. There were no niceties about it. A guy would show up off the bus and approach other guys individually or in groups, it didn't matter. He would lay out his price for a blow job or whatever was preferred. We could tell these bubbly guys usually didn't have money on their commissary account and needed to do this to get by. It wasn't flattering or altogether enticing, and I always felt a little dirty after these advances.

One boring afternoon at OKC a new bus showed up and a handful of inmates filed into our pod. One particular fellow strolled in, hips swaying and arms flailing about. His loud, tonal voice didn't cover his intentions. Sure enough, after a few hours working the pod you would see this new sister man walking around with a honey bun or fresh cup of coffee.

He would have disappeared into a cell for 20 minutes or so here and there, proving his business model successful. We happened to be a captive audience (pun intended) whose last sexual encounters were months or years in the past. It isn't an easy thing to go without sex for that long, and sooner or later lots of guys succumb to the needs and wants of the body. It isn't a new concept, but to see it happen right up front on a daily basis really jades a person and helps build a tolerance for other lifestyles. It just becomes another part of the new daily life routine that one must navigate in this controlled setting.

Some of the guys were secretive about their sexual excursions in prison and others wore it like a badge of honor. Activity like that was always easy to spot, as there are not many private places in these institutions. When I would turn down the action that was propositioned by the punks, their second question was always if I would rent out my room for a few hours instead. This is how forward it was inside, real and to the point.

A few other scenarios stood out during my waiting period at the transfer center. I had a good hour-long conversation with an Amish gentleman who was incarcerated for hate crimes within his community. Surprised by his separation of belief from personal code, I asked questions specific to his crimes, but he was keeping that information close to his vest, like a mob boss. He was, though, open to talking about his upbringing and respect for work ethic. I appreciated that. Being ignorant of their culture, I was amazed at his simplicity for want or need. I wondered to myself if this was proof that an Amish mafia does exist. That query is still up for debate.

I was also fortunate enough to endear myself to a group of about eight black gentlemen all in their 40s who watched Steve Harvey on *Family Feud* every day from 1 p.m. to 2 p.m.

during the week. One of the guys was from Kansas City, so we connected through shared interests in the Royals and Chiefs. This was a good situation to fall into because I was able to watch TV with them and kill a few hours during the day when we weren't locked in our cells. We only had limited access to the televisions after each meal. The interesting part was how they all talked so loudly at each other constantly. At first, I thought they were always upset, so I asked why they were often yelling. The response I got was one I'll never forget. One of them turned to me and without hesitation (and slight sarcasm) said, "He who is loudest is rightest." I fell in love with that answer for many reasons and became even more thankful that they let me stay in the room to watch television with them. I would sit in quiet observance as they continued to shout with their chests at one another. It was a blessing and privilege to spend time with them, as I had grown up in a rural, mostly white community, not exposed to the urban banter I sat through for weeks with them.

Well, my day finally came to gather myself and prepare for another bus ride to the next spot. At this point, I assumed that I would be moved to my Camp destination, so I was a little antsy and excited. They pulled us out around midnight, and we again went through discharge. We cuffed up, filed into another bus, and hit the road. Even though the bus was a rigid and bumpy ride, we were all in good spirits to be moving on from OKC. The guys were all rubber-necking the surrounding landscape and enjoying a sunrise that wasn't from behind a razor-wire fence. Initially, these bus rides were always a bit exciting because of the new scenery and change of routine, but this subsides after about an hour when discomfort and aching sets in. The cuffs, the company, and the COs soon snap us back to the reality of our situation. We are prisoners, not joined with the real world that we are currently being shuttled through.

Something interesting occurred to me as I realized where we were headed. Wichita was the next large city in our path, and we were traveling north on Interstate 35. I'd been on this main vein many times before. The exciting part was that north of Wichita we would drive by the city of Emporia en route to what was going to be our destination at Leavenworth, Kansas. You see, I grew up in Emporia, and a glimpse of this wonderful town from the interstate would be a heart-warming gift. These small pleasures I considered a gesture of encouragement from God to not give up the faith I had been gaining throughout the months and now years I had already spent in custody.

Sure enough, an hour and half north of Wichita we neared the college town of Emporia. Memories swam through my mind and calm soothed my soul. In the 30 seconds of viewing time that proceeded, I saw the high school I graduated from, which now seemed a lifetime ago. I also noticed the blue water towers that stood sentry over the northwest side of town as well as the water park that kept kids busy during hot summer days. I knew that I had let greed overcome me and create distance between me and this simple community. The answers were always there, I just didn't want to admit to myself that I was the problem in my own life.

I began to reflect on my situation. There was no blame to be aimed at others. Seeing Emporia reminded me of where I came from and proved that errant choices over the years had got me a seat on this bus. Choosing to do drugs created a habit for me to nurse, but choosing to then distribute drugs stirred up an appetite inside me that I wasn't prepared for. It was the ambition to succeed that eventually stung me, though. Initiative to thrive in an illegal industry is foolish and altogether risky. Greed is a real thing. We are warned against false idols and the subtleties of evil. To let our guard down is human, but to continue to do so is reckless. I sat there and reminded myself that it wasn't too late. If I continued to make the next good choice, then I could right this ship that had been off course for years.

Then it dawned on me. I started to spot homes of friends where I had spent my childhood, and it was at that moment that I quietly made a vow to myself. When I finally release from prison, I would spend as much time as I could with all the family and friends that I had avoided for so many years. Such a treat it was to see these sights, even from a prison bus. What a turning point it had been to get through all these transfers over the past 18 months. It had sunk in that I was going to make it to Leavenworth and that I could finish out the next five years there as close to home as possible.

The next few hours were still back-splitting and cramped, but the sights overshadowed the misery. I watched as we passed Topeka where I had taken my date before my first high school dance. We sped past Lawrence where I graduated from the University of Kansas. I was even able to catch a peek of Mount Oread from the highway. We exited at Bonner Springs where I attended dozens of concerts over the years at the ever-popular Sandstone Amphitheater. Visions of Tom Petty, Lenny Kravitz, and Dave Mathews all swirled through my extant mind. I wasn't home yet, but this was a big step for me in getting back to where I once belonged.

Arriving at Leavenworth was a whirlwind, and after taking several hours to get through intake/receiving I was picked up by the town driver and taken to the Camp facility down the hill from the USP. I was given a few new clothing items and a blanket and then shown to the open dorm I was assigned to.

The building was in disrepair, but the attitude was very laid back. I immediately could tell there was an easy feel in this place, more than any other prison I had been in up to this point. I didn't get shaken down by the shot-caller, I wasn't locked in a cell, and I could basically walk around the facility and yard as desired. No controlled moves. No intense questioning. Not even an overwhelming presence from the correctional officers.

I have always embraced the need to be resilient in life—in school, in jobs, in relationships, in family, in my own beliefs. Now I was able to sit on my bunk and reflect on the past 18 months I had gone through. Worry, stress, and despair started to melt away. My sentence was far from over, but I had made it to my immediate goal. When I was first sentenced to 90 months, my only concern was to be able to do that time close to home. All my actions from that point on were centered on achieving that purpose, and now it had manifested itself into this present day. I had visions of finally coming through to the end of this trek that I had begun. Today was proof and a building block on the foundation that I was constructing. Arriving at Leavenworth that day was evidence that I could come through the other side from the dark place where I once was.

This wasn't the end. It wasn't about to be stress-free days from here on out, not at all. If ever there was a time to imagine myself rising from the ashes of my former self and being handed a new beginning, then this was it. I was now able to see the days as individual building blocks. Before, my time was only about finding ways to spend each hour so I could get through to the next one. No, this was not the end. It was the genesis of something that could be beautiful again. I give God all the glory for my second start and use this as proof that lives can change. Decisions might get us to where we are now, be it satisfying or not. But it is the choices that we make going forward that will get us to where we want to go, glorious and complete.

Work assignments in prison helped me earn back my self-respect. Our community service garden project donated thousands of pounds of fresh food to those in need.

*My niece, Maclin, was born while I was in Federal Prison. Time is
the currency of life that I finally learned to appreciate and covet.
Photo from 2019.*

A CAUTIONARY TALE

"There are two important times in life.
One is the day you are born.
The other is the day you figure out why."
—Mark Twain

There was a time when a buddy of mine wanted me to front the money for a thousand ecstasy pills so he could take them down to the lake over the holiday. There he would party and sell the pills. He promised to bring me back my dollar investment and interest upon return. This guy was a friend of mine, but not a good businessman. He was social enough to move the pills, but not responsible enough to keep track of the cash. This is a typical problem in the drug trade. So I declined his offer and didn't think about his request again.

I didn't see my friend until about a week later. I wondered where he had been, but this behavior wasn't unusual since he knew people all over the metro area of KC. When he came over to my house, he seemed a little distracted or worried about something. He wouldn't look me in the face and was rather dodgy about where he'd been for the past week. I only let a few minutes pass before I directly asked him why he was acting so weird. He reluctantly admitted that he owed someone 10 grand and needed my help in fixing this problem. I was taken aback but wanted to be able to help him if possible. If it were only money that he needed, then that would be an easy fix.

But my curiosity took over and I began to question him about the situation. If I knew the person to whom he owed money, then maybe I could talk to them and help massage the situation into something reasonable. I knew enough people around Kansas City at the time that we could probably come up with a creative way to fix his folly. It would have made me more comfortable to know what my money was going toward. Gambling debt, car wreck, or something worse? I always wanted to take care of the people around me if it was for the right reasons. Since I had the means at this point in my life, then it was the least I could do. But I hated getting taken advantage of. For this reason I was always suspicious, so I usually asked a lot of questions.

My friend and I talked for several minutes so I could understand his plight in more detail. As he began to reply, I realized that he had gone over my head to my guy and asked for a loan on those thousand pills he wanted for his weekend at the lake. Two things stood out to me in this situation. One, he had disrespected and lied to me by going over my head and using my name to get his drugs. And two, he had negotiated a horrible deal on his loan. So now he wanted me to cover him for going behind my back and getting a bad deal.

I considered it briefly but decided to call my guy to sort things out instead. This way I could get both sides of the story and work on getting things squared away the best we could. We talked on the phone, and he decided to come by my place so we could discuss the problem in person. He also indicated that he was bringing a few extra guys who would wait in the car, letting me know how serious this situation was.

Before my guy got there, my friend pleaded with me to help him out of this situation. I reminded him that he already owed me thousands of dollars from similar mishaps and now he had just made things worse. I really felt bad for him and suggested he sell his car to help raise the money. I also told him I could get him a job, a real job at a hotel to start making some regular wages. He wasn't so open to either of those ideas. He only wanted me to pay my guy the $10,000 and be done with it.

His apathy and lack of responsibility was starting to wear on me. I was suspicious a lot with people in those days, and I could sense a scam getting underway.

When my guy showed up, we began to talk. I asked a few questions about quantities and quality of the product. They weren't on the same page about a lot of the details, and so I came to a few conclusions in my mind. Either they were both in on it and they were trying to hustle me for 10 grand, or my buddy was a fool and horrible with money. After deliberating for 20 minutes or so inside my Plaza apartment, we went outside. There had been enough talk at that point, and I felt it best to leave and let those two fix this suspicious quandary. I indicated that I wasn't handing over the 10 grand and they would have to figure it out for themselves.

When we finished the conversation, I walked over to my VW Passat, got inside, and drove away. I wanted to exit the situation quickly to prove to them that I wasn't going to either get scammed or help with their state of affairs, whichever one they really intended. As I looked in my rearview mirror, I saw my friend standing there with slumped shoulders. My guy was beside him, motioning toward his car where three other guys *were exiting and walking toward the two. From the looks of it, my buddy was going to get a lesson taught to him for being irresponsible with my guy's money.*

It was a bold move on my part to leave my friend behind, but in those days I made a lot of quick decisions, right or wrong—choices that were not very sympathetic to others needs and that kept my ass out of being on the wrong side of these shady dealings.

I don't know what happened to my friend that afternoon. I never spoke with him again. I believe he ended up moving to Minnesota and getting his life together. I saw my guy over the years after that, but it was never the same. He never told me what they did to my old friend, only that they threatened him to leave KC or he would never walk again. I understood the gravity of the life I was living in. That's why I was always good with my money and with other people's money. Currency was the driving motivator in this world, and violence was often the response when there was a problem with the absence of the currency. I never wanted to find out what would happen to me if I was without the drugs or the currency. God gave me the luck to stay safe.

It is a wonderful thing when life is charging forward with gusto and we maintain control with the ease of a gentle falling snow. We aren't the least bit concerned with how or why, only that it feels good. When things start to go sideways, we immediately appreciate the good times and long for their return. While doing my Fed time I went to the SHU a few times and absolutely hated it. I hadn't been mixed up in anything shady; I was just in the wrong place at the wrong time. The federal officer who ran the Education Department said to me once, "Corbin, sometimes in prison shit just happens." Well, a few times shit happened to me and off I went to the cooler. Spending time in the SHU pushed my desire for the easier times.

It was the second time I went to the SHU that I spent eight days worrying and longing to get back to the Camp. But I came out feeling a little different than before. During this stint, I was able to procure a pencil and some writing paper. I took advantage of my plight to write exactly what was on my mind. While I toiled away, frustrated because of being locked up in a small room all day long, I was able to get some feelings down on paper. It isn't the most eloquent writing ever done, but it is my truth.

Years later when I was out of prison and sitting at my mother's house reading some of my old journals, I ran across this entry. Immediately, I decided that it needed a broader audience than just me. I figured my words might help another wavering soul make some better decisions than I myself had—you know, learn from my mishaps and such. This entry is not edited for any content or context, so some of it is quite revealing. Nonetheless, it is raw and real, and I hope you appreciate it as much as I did when I first wrote it while sitting in the bucket at Leavenworth. In this entry, a rare part of me is exposed.

What do you want in life? Nice things? Good job? Loving family? Of course, a fulfilling life is enough to ask for. When does it all get to be too much? Everyone has a tipping point, and sooner or later one starts to rank important things in life and then focus more on those things that rank on the top of that list. This is a prudent process to go through and is good for initiating the achievement of happiness—concentrating on the positive.

Now, what don't you want in life? Bad health? Poverty? Misery? It is quite uneasy to start thinking about all of these things. Now, whichever we focus on, good or bad, is usually what ends up happening. You've probably heard before that your thinking manifests itself in life. There is great power within the mind, and if we take it a step further, there is great power in prayer. I bring all of this up because it is my belief that we must be careful when it comes to our intentions while entering into the spiritual realm, be it through meditation, prayer, or even self-relaxation. The world beyond us is much more powerful than you may think and especially now more than ever. I have proof.

My life has been the perfect example of a tender heart being attacked by evil. I was baptized Catholic as one of God's children in the first year of my life. Being in a good devout family, we went to Mass, learned about Jesus, and took communion. We respected people by a show of good deeds and helping others. Going to a Catholic grade school was fairly strict, but I took it all in stride by learning to live as a humble soul. I respected God, the Energy of the Universe, and the spiritual world that surrounds us here on earth.

But I, being a tender, loving heart (and maybe a bit naïve) got turned out by the world around me. For whatever reason, I would seek out approval from others. I wanted to be liked, popular with the in crowd, and a setter-of-trends in my circles. My good solid Catholic foundation took a backseat to the world . . . and I'm deeply ashamed of it. This fall happened slowly and finally started to take the biggest turns when I went away to school at the University of Kansas. It pains me to say that, because I love KU and the city of Lawrence, Kansas. I have some of my best memories from there and still love watching KU basketball and talking to KU alumni.

The University of Kansas opened my mind to many new things. There were ethics and philosophy classes, the new, exciting young people from all over the world, and the mind-expanding drugs like mushrooms and MDMA. These were all useful activities (even the drugs in moderation), but looking back I was not prepared for it all. This still tender-hearted young man started to choose the world over spiritual stability, and evil began to smile from ear to ear. One of God's own children, a lone sheep gone astray, who chose to ignore the Universe's signs to be led back into God's loving hands. This isn't necessarily a unique story, but it's my story of hope and salvation in the most dire of circumstances.

You see, I must explain something to you. What I'm about to tell you is the truth from the bottom of my heart. God spoke to me at quite a young age. These are my earliest memories and my proof (if only to myself) of my special place in God's Kingdom.

When I was several months old, I was baptized in Wichita, Kansas. This is typical of a newborn in a Roman Catholic family. I remember this event, personally. Not from pictures or others telling me stories about it, but I have vivid memories of my father handing me over to a priest and dousing my forehead in Holy Water. The priest made the sign of the cross and I cried like a baby, literally. Now, I didn't know what it meant at the time, but I know God spoke to me. A light shined all around me and the Creator of the Universe made it clear that I was blessed. It's peculiar that these memories would be with me from such a young age, but it is the sincere truth.

The feeling that great things were in store for me hung with me throughout childhood. I understand that most kids think they are special, and I'd say that they certainly are. I had been consecrated into God's own family, but I didn't know what that meant. Was there to be a good life in front of me? Wealth? Success? Happiness? Yes, these things were all possible.

But a gentle heart should never stray too far from home. Well, I did just that. Thinking I was strong in the world and seeking its favor, I struck out to conquer all that I could. Forgetting one's foundation is a huge character flaw. It wasn't my parents or friends or upbringing. Being one of God's children and then choosing the world over everlasting life has nearly ruined me several times. Free will is the biggest responsibility we have as humans, and sin can sure give free will a bad name.

When evil recognizes a stray sheep and has the potential to bring disaster upon virtuous living, then evil attacks with all its might. This is where our flaws come into play. Here it is determined that what we focus on affects our lives. One of my weaknesses is that my worry and internal anxieties take over my thinking to the extent of external failure. Basically, as I grew older I began to fear things more, worry about them, and then manifest them into my life. This is what got me where I am today—in a rough spot. That's right, as I write this I am not at the pinnacle of enjoyment in my life. No, I haven't overcome the bad circumstances I got myself into in order to regain my place in God's chosen army. That is the paradox I struggle with at this very moment.

Here is where I sit. Skipping forward a dozen years or so after college, I got put in federal prison for drug distribution. Evil worked in me to turn this once man of Christ into a lustful, greedy, seeker of worldly favor. I had many idols other that God. Money, women, drugs, cars, popularity, all the typical things that a lost soul puts ahead of God. Well, a federal indictment basically removes everything in your life. The demons that ran my days *were enormously proud that they had taken a devout soldier and stripped him bare. God gave me signs all along the way, but my focus in life had become skewed. My goals were so different than when I was young and an up-and-coming soldier for the love of the universe. That is how the evil one fights God. He gets to good people, like he got to me, and steals them away from God's grace. It's a shame, but that's what is scary about the world.*

Here is where my initial warning signs come into play. In jail, I turned back to God. I write about what that process was, and I am eternally thankful for God giving me the wisdom to seek His favor and forgiveness. Here's the troubling part that I am living through right now. In seeking God anew, humbly, and with earnest might, I have angered the evil who has been admiring the work it had achieved in my life. The harder I now seek out God and His teachings, the more confident I become in the authenticity of the spiritual war that is going on. In repledging my life to being a soldier of God, it has brought me deeper into a daily battle of Biblical proportions. I rebuilt my spiritual foundation. I attend Mass, respect the sacraments, pray constantly, study spirituality, and wholeheartedly work on all the things that will bring me closer to God. I am willing to die for Him. I yearn to be a soldier for Him in my afterlife because God told me that was my purpose on the day when I was baptized.

Problem is, I'm still human and weak in the flesh. I may have stopped using drugs, started loving others around me, and diligently pledged my services to God every day, but I'm just a guy. I must fulfill my purpose as a soldier of Christ.

The last thing I'm working on is my anxiety, my worrying mind, and Satan hasn't just turned tail to quit. No, he realizes that he can still hurt this tender heart in this life and is doing everything he can to eat me up. He sure is angry with me.

Fortunately, at this point, I have recognized my weaknesses but haven't overcome them. He entered into my apprehension and is trying to turn me away from God. This is what I mean when I say be careful when spending time in the spiritual realm. What I have gone through would nearly wreck most people. Drug addiction to the extreme, dodging murder and death on several occasions, mental-health breakdowns that should have institutionalized me, and a time of lonely despair where I spent hundreds of thousands of dollars to self-medicate the problem. Some of it will shock you. It still shocks me, and I lived through it.

The world is changing quickly and the spiritual realm surrounding us is having a more tremendous effect on our daily lives. It may be that the rapture will soon be upon us, that there is a changing progressive consciousness around the world, or the collective search for more meaning in life itself. Whatever the case, we should indeed love God with all our heart, and all our soul, and our entire mind, and all our being. Beyond that, we need to be prepared for all that entails. Remember, this world isn't fair, and everyone's experience will be different.

This world is also temporary, and the only things we take with us into eternity are our character and faith. Not our resumé or all the tools in our garage. Not the business we've built, or even our favorite jacket. Once you accept this, things can get difficult. They sure did for me. This is the precautionary attitude that I'm suggesting you take.

As I indicated, with all your being, love God. Period. But be ready for the life changes that arise, because evil hates good. However, God loves good and good trumps evil every time. Easily. I will admit that my path to get to God this second time around has been a chore. It's a goal that I keep on seeking to fill the emptiness in my life. Blind ambition may be fueling this search, but I've grown tired of the things the world has to offer. I pray without ceasing for the glory of the afterlife. I want Heaven and I want it now. For whatever reason, God still has me on this earth when there have been dozens of opportunities for me to drift away into mediocrity. Hence, I press on ... on to the next thing.

I suggest you press on as well. This tale is intended to get you ready for the next great steps in your life, should you choose to take them. Be grounded, firm in your intentions, and cast your worries aside. Only let the beautiful things manifest themselves in your life. This isn't a recipe for success or a formula for wealth. These are the ingredients to purpose in life, so pay attention. Take notice of your choices; don't get caught in a whirlwind, as so many of us have. You will most assuredly want to be aligned with the energy of the universe as you figure it all out.

So, the saga continues . . .

When I read this several years after I had first written it, the thoughts that came over me were that I was inspired by stress. The discomfort of being locked in a small room all day and night. A person adjusts to their surroundings, but the first several days of being shoved into a concrete box were mind-cramping. The weight of the walls, the thick smell of wet metal, and the schizophrenic lighting added to my discontent. I worried about the outcome. The mind considers how events could have gone differently. The body struggles between choosing to relax or to take a sprint through the bolted cell door. All the things you want to do, but cannot, had scurried wildly through my brain, and then what came out is what I wrote above.

I was also pleased when I looked through it again after so many years because it was real. Genuine feelings unedited. Raw emotions. I knew, at the time, I had attempted to write as cordially as possible—knowing deep down that I wanted this to be part of a manuscript that I would put together some day. I had realized in myself that I took my time like a man. In the interest of closure from that part of my life, I gave my pound of flesh to the Bureau of Prisons and, more importantly, to God. So in that moment, I decided to move forward with my life, to stay away from what I did on the streets years before. Yes, it was pleasing to know that I would get through it by following the advice from my own *Cautionary Tale.*

During my sentence, when I was locked up in a cell alone for weeks or months at a time, it was writing that rescued me. The scribbling of notes on whatever paper I could get my hands on. I often sharpened the pencil on a jagged piece of metal protruding from the old door that kept me blocked from any semblance of reality. I even remember running out of paper and using that short pencil to write on the concrete walls that surrounded me. Not graffiti or drawings, but choice words of inspiration and love. Prayers, thoughts, hopes, and advice jotted down for anyone else who might run across them in the future. It was more therapy for me personally, but these fragments mended a broken puzzle of memories for me to build upon.

Scouring over these notes years later helped me realize I was building a foundation that could be unshakable if I allowed it. Writing, for me, turned out to be a way of learning and an opportunity for teaching myself. The things I would write were scattered thoughts and intentions. But when written, I was solidifying my purposes and making tangible what I had been learning over time. Whether it was readings from the Bible, teachings from Eastern philosophy, or texts by Stephen Hawking, I absorbed it and regurgitated it on paper with the best understanding I could. For whatever reason, the times I was under the most stress are when I composed my most meaningful thoughts.

I found headings in my old notes that stated, "Being a good person doesn't get you into Heaven," "How it worked," and "Thirst, ever-quenched." What followed these headings were more writings—stressed thoughts really. Some delved into my own mystic beliefs, which actually surprised me. I was pleased that some of these ideas had made it to paper where I could now continue these thoughts from a different perspective. Other writings expressed frustration with the system I was caught up in and the evil that found its way into many of the humans working within it.

Another intriguing excerpt is one that I found titled, "Where is Jesus now?" Following are the first few paragraphs, again unedited. It is fresh, written from a dark, discouraged, and lonely corner of the Special Housing Unit at Leavenworth USP. Notice, though, that there is hope. It uncovers an understanding that struggle will find us and knock us out of our square. But a desire that comes from trust and belief in a power greater than ourselves can carry us through to a stronger place and on to the next thing.

Where is Jesus now?

A countless many books have been written about this great man we all know. God Himself manifested His energy as a human being on our humble planet so we could have a better understanding of why we are here. Why do we exist at all? If you are reading this, then you probably have a greater yearning for and belief in what our ultimate purpose here is. What a great example Jesus was and still is to us. His actions spoke volumes for His intentions while His spoken word was nothing short of awe-

inspiring. I am infinitely thankful for the sacrifices He made so that we humans could live with the all-powerful energy of the universe after our worldly lives are over. All we have to do is believe. Have faith and understand that each of our souls is special to God, His love is forever.

Now, we have times in our lives when despair, anxiety, worry, and temptation control our being and we ask ourselves, "Where is Jesus now?" I won't pretend to understand God's mighty ways, but I do accept them. Our actions in this world do affect the spiritual realm around us. I take comfort in knowing that working through trials and tribulations are strengthening my place in the afterlife. If I struggle now and still praise God all the while, then the glory that waits for me grows exponentially. So when times are hard, I continue to persevere. I will admit that it isn't easy, the human flesh is weak. The more we live in Christ, the more evil tries to bring us down. The dark knows what we fear the most and it will do anything to keep us from loving God.

James 1:2-3 Take joy in various trials because we know that testing of one's faith produces perseverance and strength.

It is only fitting that we find strength again in life, even if we are forced to use our own foolishness as building blocks. For me, it was bad decisions such as avoiding responsibilities and being selfish in relationships. Couple those with drug use and working in a black-market economy, and they all earned me a trip to prison so I could straighten myself out again. I got so far away from who I was supposed to be in life that it seemed only proper to be slingshot around back to square one. It is the hard route to take, but I needed to experience all the bad, the entirety of the negative, to get back to the right side of life again.

Not everyone needs devastating events to occur for a wake-up call. If these chapters can enlighten just a few people, then I'm sure the ripple effect could be inspiring. Getting to the SHU in Leavenworth never crossed my mind when I was making wrong decisions in succession. The thought of being moved to eight different institutions over the course of 18 months frightened me. The idea of being locked in small rooms for weeks on end gave nausea a new meaning. But here I am sharing the complete truth of my experiences, exclaiming two things to you now:

1. Trust in something larger than yourself.
2. Use that trust to make the right decisions in life.

It isn't always easy or apparent right away what you should do, but undertaking the appropriate deed isn't always a snap decision. Most everyone has a conscience. When there's an energy bigger that you as the guide, then your principles can be counted on as moral.

Where is Jesus now? Taking us through each route in life. Not every course is easy, but each is joyous if seen from the perspective that we are being made more complete. Ordeals and even misfortunes can be turned into opportunities for growth if only the mind is kept steady, and we see these tribulations for what they are—training for the rest of our life and everything thereafter.

A photo of me (Corbin) driving around The Country Club Plaza doing my deliveries. On that day I thought the money was worth the anxiety and pain it caused in my life.

Always up to some kind of mischief when I was living fast in 2009.

DAYS LIKE NO OTHERS

"One day your life will flash before your eyes.
Make sure it is worth watching."
—Gerard Way

Here shadows a glimpse into the most typical of days in Leavenworth Federal Prison Camp, following me from sunup to sundown. This facility provided me the most "freedom," as we were not locked down much and some of us were able to leave the dorms to go work on the grounds of the prison compound during the day. My description is a little draggy at times on purpose to give the reader a true feel of how time pulls along at a tractor's pace while inside doing a stint. It was six years of suck that I will never get back. It was six years of revival that I appreciate even more than I hated it.

###

A dreamful sleep is delightful, especially in a place where finding solitude can be like grasping smoke spiraling from a fire. This is why waking up and seeing the same concrete wall that you have seen hundreds of mornings in a row is still a shock to the soul. It certainly lets you appreciate the distant voyage you were adventuring on just moments before. The dream is one of the only escapes in prison, and mornings are always the most grueling time for me, a reminder that I am still living in a human warehouse.

So when I wake up in prison, I roll around for a few minutes, contemplate my own existence, and reminisce on the dreams that now seem all too fleeting. A shame. It took me years to unriddle the repetition of dwelling on my sorrows and station. After a chunk of time, I just convinced myself to man up and dive into the grind of doing another day. I watched hundreds of guys that I share this facility with get up and fumble around about their day. I finally just stared in the mirror one evening and said to myself, "Surely I can figure this out." So the first choice of the day is if I want to get up early enough to make it to breakfast in the chow hall. It's a meal, it's free, and they might even have an apple or a decent breakfast cake to nibble on. Whatever the case, it's the first thing on the agenda to get me through another day.

I decide to flop out of my bunk, quietly enough to not disturb my bunkmate if he's still asleep. In a place like prison, it isn't good to wake up another guy intentionally or unintentionally. The whole dream thing, ya dig? It's important to the serenity of existence in prison. He may be enjoying his own temporary escape, where he is far away from here and visiting old friends or loved ones.

Immediately, I notice that he is already up, respectfully sitting up on his bunk quietly in the dark. It's hard to find a good bunkmate in these places, and when you do it's a blessing. I've been lucky to have a run of several over the years. Charlie works at the recycling facility here at Leavenworth and is getting his boots on, dressing in his issued khakis, and gathering his necessary gear for work. Gloves, a hat, and a folder with some papers he wants to copy. I think they are some pictures he has drawn, and the duplicates he will send home to his family. Nothing special though, just another morning in this institutional setting.

I change out of my sleeping shorts and put on my issued uniform as well. My garden boots are floppy and worn, while my socks are thin and scuzzy. Two pairs are necessary, as I'll be working outdoors today. So many of my clothing items have little life left in them.

I gear up immediately; it's just easier that way. This is my first calibration into the day. There is no comfortable couch for me to lounge on or kitchen table to gather at anyhow, only benches and metal countertops. If I get up and ready myself immediately, then it helps force me to move on to the next thing, you see. This assists my adjustment into living another day in the custody of the federal government.

So, preparing for the day starts with a trip down the hall to the bathroom. Along the way, I pass the shower stalls where one shower is spilling water, occupied by a large Hispanic gentleman. The other showers are empty but still smell like a steamy mop closet.

The lights are dim, and my somber mood agrees with the other inmates.

Two short, stout Mexican guys stand sentry outside the shower room, peering at a line of three other guys waiting to get in for their morning wash. This is actually fairly common. The large guy gets the showers to himself when he is in there, and he has the other guys standing watch to make sure nobody else bothers him during his morning ritual. The other guys in the hallway wait until he is finished and exited until they are able to pile in and continue on with their respective days. Each of us carve out our little corner of the universe and cater it to what is important to us as individuals. This guy cherishes the time during his morning shower so much that he pays his buddies (probably with postage stamps) to stand guard so he gets his privacy in there.

I walk past that scene and into the sink room to splash some water on my face. Mind you, it's about 5:45 a.m. Turning the corner, I spy a group of about seven black gentlemen—guys mostly younger than me—all mingling in and around the small room. I look to use one of the seven sinks while they are chatting up a storm, a lively exchange for this hour of the day.

I notice that they are in here this morning twisting and braiding each other's hair. I learned about the motivations for different hairstyles in prison, although I just usually kept mine short and easy to manage. This hair ritual is a normal occurrence; I'm simply curious as to why it's happening before the first light of day. Regardless, it's just representative of another event that is usually sprinkled throughout a typical day in a prison. One becomes accustomed to the strange and unusual, almost like living in a fraternity for grown men.

The guys in the sink room don't bother me as I slide next to one of the sinks and throw some water on my face and hair. A quick little bird bath along with a brushing of the teeth. The same thing I do every morning, only with whatever random happenings that might be going on in a place where hundreds of guys share the same hallway and restrooms. The more years one spends in a place like this, the less shocking it becomes, and normalcy borders the unexpected.

After getting put together, I scurry over to the chow hall and get in line for breakfast. It's almost always oatmeal, canned fruit, or an apple (if we are lucky), milk, and some sort of sugary cake that is low grade and not good for you. I eat it some of the time just to change things up, but I'm not in the mood today. I try and eat as healthy as possible in this place because I want to get out one day and be in decent shape. By the time I get back to society, I'll have a lot of catching up to do. So I generally eat the oatmeal and put some of the cake in it for flavor, just a little.

Pulling up to the chow hall, I see about 50 guys in front of me in line, so I file in like a good inmate. I look to see who the CO is that is running the chow hall this morning and notice it's a decent guy, so I put my headphones in and keep to myself in formation. Some of the COs won't let you listen to your radio or even have headphones in your ears in the chow hall. Each boss has a different set of unwritten rules that we have to learn to abide by. It takes time to figure these things out, but I've been in Leavenworth for years now.

With my headphones in I can look up at the TV on the wall and listen to the morning news. If I tune in to the corresponding station, then my radio picks up whatever station is showing on that particular TV. Perfect. I am not very social in the morning, even bordering on withdrawn, so being able to spend the next 20 minutes eating my oatmeal in peace and staring at the news is a win for me.

Inching my way closer in line toward the serving station, I survey my surroundings. Some guys are barely awake, hair askew with eyes still red and swollen. They are quiet and just want a muffin to fill the void in their stomach this morning. Others are loud, near yelling in conversation and standing only a few feet from each other. Comical? No. Entertaining? Slightly. It's only because they are oblivious to their own ignorance and the content of their conversation. Something about babies' mammas and needin' that 'skrilla to get them new chips in the commissary. I suppose they are having their conversation loud enough for everyone to hear just in case someone wanted to donate to their worthy cause.

After making my way through the line, I find my usual table and chair. I call it mine because after being institutionalized for several years one gets accustomed to routine and normalcy. It is comforting to know that I can sit at this chair and look at the TV from this place in the chow hall—a vantage point that I like. Not right underneath it, but close enough to still read the ticker at the bottom of the screen.

A few people I know sit nearby and we exchange pleasantries. The guys I hang out with in here are good dudes. We always make sure to keep each other held up but also respect each other's space, especially in the morning. These relationships just happen over time, years anyhow, of being around the same people. We learn how to keep our shared surroundings as comfortable as possible.

One guy, John, asks if I need any help at the garden today. He isn't busy at his work assignment and would like to come out to help and keep distracted for a few hours. I like John. He's from Kansas City, so we have enough in common to have spirited conversations. We also play music together, as he is getting better and better on the piano. I accompany his piano playing with my guitar skills. We both arrived here three years ago at about the same time, so we've been on this journey for a bit now. We know how to be around each other and recognize respectful boundaries.

I respond that I could sure use some help out there, always can. We'll be harvesting sweet corn that is donated to a local charity, and an extra set of hands will help us get through the heat quicker. We don't chat a whole lot more, as I feel like getting back to my calm TV watching, so he turns his conversation to our friend Aaron who also sits nearby.

I'm able to spend a few peaceful minutes watching the news before I become distracted by some guys sitting at a table next to me. They seem to be aged in their 50s and look a bit burned out from the years they've been down. I can hardly blame them.

My distraction is because they are ogling over the newscaster woman—how hot she is and what they wouldn't do to her, etc. It's early in the morning and they are sexualizing a fully clothed woman on the news. It's just another reminder of how sensory deprived we are in here, and I become a little sad.

To shed some light on the situation, I politely get their attention and point them in the direction of the Spanish language TV set up on the other end of the chow hall. There are about 20 Spanish-speaking guys over there all staring blankly at the news show playing on Telemundo. I motion toward the weather gal giving the latest forecast for the Miami area. Yes, many of us are familiar with what weather ladies wear on Hispanic channels, similar to something one might see her in at a club on a Saturday night. Instinctively, the two gents get up and move to continue their breakfasts in front of the Spanish-speaking TV, joining the gazes of the other inmates watching. The weather report this morning sees no language or color barriers.

As I finish my food and approach the kitchen to drop off my empty tray to the dishwasher, I chat with Aaron for a minute. He's a liberal guy from Nebraska who is good for some open-minded conversation and genuine companionship while doing grunt work out in the hot sun. We agree on picking some sweet corn this afternoon and decide to meet at the greenhouse, where we will gather the other inmates who volunteer their time.

Working at the garden is hard and dirty work but not without its rewards. It has been a place to steer clear of the guards who roam the halls and bark orders during the daytime hours. Besides avoiding the oppression of the prison, we also get a sense of accomplishment because of the people who benefit from our food donations throughout the summer.

I slip out of the chow hall with an apple hidden in my pocket, a nice mid-morning snack. This is not allowed, taking food out of the chow hall, even though it was issued to me. Guys are always wrapping food up in napkins and smuggling it out like bandits, but today is different. The associate warden happens to be standing right outside the chow hall doors and yelps in my direction. "You there! Inmate! Empty your pockets! Nothing leaves the chow hall!" There's no arguing with the guy, so I simply head his direction, tail between my legs. I place the apple in the trash can next to him and apologize. He stares rigidly for a few seconds and then waves me away as he says, "You know better than that!" I do, and he is right. This is his world; I'm just passing through it. He should be proud for saving the prison from sure disaster. I've learned not to try and make sense of the rules, only to follow them or be prepared for the consequences. In this instance, an apple in the trash has been a risk I was willing to take.

Finally, the virtuous part of the day is about to begin. I get to walk out to the greenhouse and then work at the garden. Several of us have a work assignment out there. It's a great respite from the crap hole we live in, and as long as we are back in our dorms for 4 p.m. count, we're able to continue with the projects we have going. The garden is on prison property behind the Leavenworth Hot House, so it is hidden from sight to most of the general public. We work 30 acres and much of the labor is done by hand—think old plantation-style organic farming. It wouldn't be feasible in the real world to have a working farm like this, but with our monthly wages being in the 20-dollar range, they can surely afford our efforts and results.

This Community Service Garden Project is set up in conjunction with the local Lion's Club. The surrounding community donates seeds and materials, while the inmates grow the food on the prison grounds. The food is in turn donated back to community groups who stop by twice weekly during summer months to pick up the harvest. The program is one of the few bright spots here, and I am secretly proud to be a part of something where my efforts reach further than myself. I feel that the hard work is a penance that I am paying for the wrongs I committed in the past. This work out here is my real sentence, not the living in squalor that figures my existence inside the prison walls.

It is about a half mile walk to the greenhouse which doubles as our shop and hangout, for lack of a better description. The heat inside is variable, depending on the weather, and the rain causes it to leak in about 25 different places. There's a small desk in there, four chairs, and some tables to work at. When the wind blows, I worry if today will be the day that we are whisked away to the land of Oz. It is pretty run down, but it's ours and we appreciate it for what it is.

As I'm leaving the main building of the prison Camp, I notice two inmates who are assigned to work at the paint shop walking back into the building with five-gallon buckets in each hand. I know immediately that they are not preparing for a long day of painting walls in the facility. Nobody is ever so motivated first thing in the morning to get ready for actual work in this place. Over time, I've learned that most everything you see is not what it appears on the surface. One inmate once told me to believe half of what I see and none of what I hear. This situation fits exactly into that train of thought.

These two guys from the paint department were smuggling something into the prison. What it was, I don't know for sure. It could simply be some sort of food that's not available to us inside or something more nefarious such as drugs or even weapons. Whatever the case, these five-gallon paint buckets were part of whatever caper they were involved in at that time. It is none of my business, so I keep on walking and try to pay it no mind. Probably best to not even ask questions or acknowledge that you notice, or you may get labeled a snitch. Once you get that title in here, it's hard to shake. You will get treated like crap, and it makes your time that much more difficult. There's no reason to be more miserable in an already dismal existence.

During the walk up to the greenhouse, I pass the welding shop, landscaping department, and the metal recycling building, where many other inmates are assigned to work. Those working at these respective spots also get to leave the compound during work hours. The understanding is that we have fairly good job assignments here in prison, as good as can be expected in our otherwise dull reality.

I say hello to a few of the others as we are all filing out in the same direction. A chorus of single word grunts dominates the exchanges between us all this morning. "Okay, alright," followed by a "Yep, I see you," is about as deep as the communications get right now. Most of us have been doing this for some years now and we see one another constantly, so there's not a whole lot of catching up to do. Besides, it's overkill to get jazzed up for another day on the job in a federal prison. With too many smiles, mocking or shaming might follow.

I do see my friend Brad (not his real name) along the way and we briefly chat. He is a spiffy-looking, middle-aged guy here on some white-collar money laundering charges. We took some drug counseling classes together and play a little tennis in the evenings to pass the time. As we agree to catch up tonight on the court, I recall that he is much better than I am, but if we play doubles, then I might have a chance to best him and his partner in a set or two. Seems like a decent enough plan, something to look forward to after 4 p.m. count.

Making my way into the greenhouse, the sun is just peeking through the plastic windows and several lazy farmers are sprawled out mumbling about tractors and tillage. Their conversation seems surface level and dull from the outside, but I can tell that these sorts of exchanges comfort them in a place where they certainly do not fit in. Overall, these are some good dudes, hard workers, and smart common-sense fellows who got caught up in some nonsense that put them here, away from anything that resembles normal. I recognize that these typical talks about their work back in the real world distract them from where they really are and help them.

Additionally, I can tell they really don't enjoy working with me because I've been here for years and the federal officer in charge of our department considers me his number one go-to guy for running this garden. Never mind that I had no experience in this sort of thing before coming here, but

I'm years into it now and it has helped me stay involved in something meaningful while doing this time.

But what self-respecting lifetime farmer wants to work alongside a novice who disperses the marching orders from our boss. I get it, but I don't care what they think. This is how I do my time, and I'm not going to let them mess with that if I can help it.

Okay, here is what baffles me about how a typical morning meeting goes with these fine gentlemen. We all exchange pleasantries and comment on the weather. It's another hot and humid one, typical of a July day in Kansas. We then discuss how the farm is doing, what needs harvested, what needs cultivated, plans for fall plantings, and, most urgently, what is getting overrun by weeds and needs cleaned up. I tell them I have some guys coming out to help pick corn in the afternoon and suggest we should all spend an hour getting some tomatoes harvested this morning. Fair enough. Makes sense. They nod in agreement, say that sounds fine, and comment that the tomatoes look good and are coming along nicely.

So we all spend the next 10 or 15 minutes getting hydrated, gathering up baskets, and loading the trailers. Then, as I get on the tractor and begin to head to the field toward the tomato section, I see the farmers walking off in another direction. It looks like they are maybe going to the landscape department or who knows. Without another word, they disappear for the morning to go fix lawn mowers or play with the welding equipment. It really doesn't matter to me one way or another. I always believe, especially in this place, that people should do whatever they want to do. Grown adults make their own decisions. The confusing part is that only minutes ago I understood that we were all going down to pick tomatoes together, and now they had gone off in another direction.

I know what you are thinking—they pulled the 'ol "okey doke" on me and played me for a fool just to get out of helping me for the day. Well, not exactly true. I had these guys pegged when they walked in the door of the prison. Newbies, out of their element and looking for a place to hide for the next several years while they did their time. This way, they could fall under the radar of the main prison's rampaging annoyances.

Great! Wonderful. Hide out here, I'm all for that. But for grown men to sit there and talk words around in circles, well, this just isn't the place for that. So I learn that in prison, even the good 'ol boys are flakes and exaggerators. Just another reason why a lot of guys get out of this place jaded and tired of people. Living up close and personal to a bunch of fakes and talkers is tiresome on the soul.

Well, I spend the remainder of the morning picking tomatoes with my only other comrade, a Spanish man in his 60s named Murillo. I enjoy working with him very much. He is wise, respectful, asks good questions, and is good at doing time in prison. He and I have been out here together working for a few years now, so we understand each other's habits and limits of joking around, and, most importantly, we have avoided annoying one another over the years. I'd rather just work with Murillo anyhow; the farmers know too much for their own good and couldn't just relax and accept the hardships we have for what they are. Murillo understands that we have to just do the best we can with what we have without complaining that we are without so many things that can make our lives easier.

It is humid, even in the morning, so we are taking regular breaks under the only tree nearby. During these breaks I begin thinking about all the clichés in prison and how close to the truth they really are. This is why my buddies and I in here will always say, "Well ... on to the next thing." It's our way of saying, "See ya later!" It's a supporting gesture claiming that yes, we are all in this together and we'll keep moving forward together. The next thing is all we can do—all we can control. I like our little proverb, and it makes us all feel closer. It's as if our time here is still meaningful even though deep down we all know that every day we are missing out on real life events that lay beyond our grasp. Getting ourselves on to the next thing is all that we can do to keep our own sanity.

Murillo and I chat as we chew on some fresh tomatoes and gulp down plenty of water on our breaks. He, too, recognizes the inconsistencies with the farmers and agrees to just let them do whatever it is that they enjoy doing. We could sure use the help out here in the tomatoes—a thousand plants, probably two acres full. It's the most tomato plants I have ever grown at once, more than I ever care to see again. But it is a great way to spend the day, rather than being locked in a confined space. I respect my friend who is helping me out here today and will genuinely miss him when we finally get to leave this place and venture back home to our families. I hope he gets back to his ranch in Mexico and lives out the remainder of his life cooking, smiling, and playing with his grandchildren.

These pleasant visions are suddenly interrupted as we spot an officer-issued truck approaching us. I look up and already know that it is the SIS team, a group of prison guards that act as the actual cops or detectives on the compound. They spend their time going around searching departments and making sure inmates are not getting involved in anything counter to the orderly operation of the facility. They often come to search out here because it is outside the compound proper and can be a good place for contraband to get stashed, hidden, exchanged, or smoked. Regardless, I'm familiar with these searches and only somewhat bothered by them these days. It's more like an annoying formality, such as listening to your boss brag about his most recent vacation to Vegas. "You just wouldn't get it unless you were there, man!"

Seeing this truck pull toward us reminds me of certain consequences that may occur when these correctional officers show up; dealing with these guys can be annoying. If an inmate is really up to something, then their arrival can get him put in the SHU or written up with an incident report, or they will simply make your stay at Camp Leavenworth uncomfortable. I always say to the other guys out here that this is, "Reason number (insert whatever number you want here) why you shouldn't come to prison." So when one of these guards shows up and wants to search you, we simply smirk and mutter to each other, "Well, reason number 117 why we shouldn't have come to prison." It's a lame saying, but it never really gets old in here. One of the few things that has some staying power. That and the shaming. The guards enjoy talking down to us inmates for their own amusement.

Speaking of clichés, I have never seen such typical prison guards in my life. I couldn't have created them out of all the prison movie scenes I've watched over the years. They have the official blue button-ups with the backward American flag on the sleeve. (I never understood why they couldn't have just put it going the correct direction on the opposite sleeve or switched it to go the direction we're all used to seeing on this sleeve.) I suppose this goes along with why I came to believe that BOP stood for backwards on purpose.

Their shirts are unkempt, unbuttoned at the bottom, and

falling out over their belted pants, which are too tight around the waist. They speak to me in a rowdy rumble as if I might be amused by their enthusiasm. I will never understand their haste to search inmates, to rub up and down on men's bodies all day probing for an excuse to write out a shot or incident report. They were also sweaty, grubby, and looking for a reason to get us caught up in something if they could.

It's always smart to be respectful and not too talkative. Short, pointed answers that don't give them reasons to ask you more questions. Also, be aware. Don't give yourself or any other inmates up in your conversations with them. They are not your friends, simply your captors that you must get along with for the years that you are housed in prison.

I immediately assume the position with arms spread up from my sides, legs apart, and eyes fixed forward. The most difficult part is to not stare at their neck rolls or get distracted by their labored breathing. At one point, I think I hear Billy Bob Thornton from *Sling Blade* grunting behind me. *Uhhmm huh.*

Murillo and I are both clean, and they tell us to sit down for the next 10 minutes as they search our vehicle (the tractor) and trailer. We offer them some tomatoes, but they insist that they are not interested in eating anything unless it is something that is fried, ice cream, or fried ice cream. Anything fresh is certainly out of the question.

Getting searched in prison gets to be as typical as taking a peek inside the fridge just to see what's in there. It can be daily, or even multiple times a day. The searches don't bother me, even when they tear up my locker and small cell/living space. When they do that, it reminds me of children throwing a tantrum, embarrassing for sure.

The only part that discourages me is when we get talked to

slimy or dirty, like we are really slaves or lesser forms of human beings. Do they forget that we are all American citizens? We are NOT terrorists. Most importantly, we are getting out of prison one day and will live in normal neighborhoods among society, possibly next door to one of them. So to talk to us like we pooped in their cereal is beyond me, but this also becomes just like everything else in here. We endure it to the end, the bitter end.

They toss some of our things around and ask us what we are doing. I assume it is obvious that having a trailer with baskets full of tomatoes speaks for itself, but they must be waiting for us to say something else. Maybe they want us to answer that we are cooking crystal meth or smuggling in cell phones. I see nothing, I admit to nothing! But I do offer them some tomatoes one more time even though they decline once again.

Before they leave, one of them gets up in my face real close, so I can smell the Skoal on his chops. He stares at me really good and says, "I'm keepin' my eye on ya's ... so you's better keep it clean out here. No drugs, no phones, no porn." I am amused, don't get me wrong, but also feel a little dirty. Does he really think I'm out here in a field of tomatoes getting weird on some porn? I *have* been locked up for some years, but if I'm going to do any pleasuring of myself, it will be in the privacy of the institutional showers, thank you very much! I keep this conversation in my head and instead tell him that all activities are business as usual out here. No problems, be assured. Our interaction goes as well as to be expected, and we are all worse off for wear. Nevertheless, we're able to proceed with our morning now.

It's hard to imagine a much different day up to this point. Only 10:30 in the a.m. registers on the sundial and most of the typical events in prison have already occurred. Why, whatever will we do to keep ourselves entertained for the rest of the day?

We decide this is a good stopping point for the time being and talk about gathering some food to prepare for lunch.

Don't get me wrong, we are extremely lucky to be working out here at the farm. Abundant fresh produce is at our fingertips, and we can eat whatever we want. Fresh squash, zucchini, tomatoes, peppers, potatoes, eggplant, melons, okra, greens. All these things we are able to pick, mix up, and microwave into a healthy midday meal. I will buy a bag of sardines off the commissary for a buck and mix it in for some protein to keep my stomach full. This is my typical lunch during the summer months when the garden is running at full capacity.

Now, the availability of this fresh produce is something that we treasure since it's such a perk in a place like this. Most guys trek back to the compound to eat lunch in the chow hall. By doing this they subject themselves to searches, heckling from inmates and staff, dead tasteless food, and the general annoyances of eating with hundreds of other bothersome people. By gathering some fresh food and heading back to the greenhouse to use the microwave that we have hidden in there, Murillo and I can eat in peace and wait for our afternoon crew to meet us out here for our sweet corn harvest. We also gather several melons to snack on and to share with any other inmates we see along the way. This little bit of allocation helps create appreciation among the other guys since fresh cantaloupe isn't something easy to come by in our segregated society, otherwise known as LVC.

Back at the greenhouse we sit in the shade and enjoy our lunches. From our seats here, we have a vantage point that lets us see up and down an access road. This road gets used by the different facilities departments to move from place to place outside the compound. Since we are housed in a minimum-security Camp facility, most of the upkeep and maintenance for the larger USP Leavenworth is done by inmates from the Leavenworth Camp facility. Mowing the grounds, taking care of electrical repairs, painting, welding, plumbing, and food service—any skill needed to keep a mini-town up and running has a department within this federal compound. The inmates are able to check out vehicles for official use and traverse this gravel road during work hours. There are also BOP administrators, prison guards, and department heads driving on this road. Murillo and I sit and observe the action as we nibble on our healthy eats. It becomes quite entertaining some days when we finally understand what is really happening with all the traffic.

You see, most guys in prison have some sort of side hustle going on. Since the majority of jobs pay 20 bucks or less a month, many of us come up with ways to supplement our income. This can be as simple as trading a cantaloupe for some electrical tape when needed. This is the type of bartering I get into. Minor and insignificant really. But oftentimes the stakes are much higher with whatever hustle these guys around here have working. One must remember, we didn't get put in federal prison for petty theft and parking tickets. Many of these men had elaborate scams and criminal networks working around them for years before getting caught up. Just because they are behind bars now doesn't mean that their line of thinking and means of acquiring currency has changed. The only difference is where they are and how they go about it.

Having this opportunity to sit for 30–45 minutes and just observe what happens on this access road often keeps us plugged into the rumor mill. Many times, we see things that we really don't want any part of. For example, we may watch two eminent individuals who are assigned to the plumbing department with a truck full of tools. They can be seen driving around and checking some of the water lines throughout the compound. One of the lines just happens to be near some public roads. From a distance we may see them pull up the truck, gather their large bags full of "tools" out of the back of the truck and run over to check a line. There will be a period of rummaging around, and after a short time they'll scurry back to the truck throwing the large bags of "tools" in the back. Then we'll see the truck speed to the rear gate of the compound where they will drive near the back entrance of one of the housing units. Here, they will stop the truck again, toss the bags out, and speed away just as quickly as they arrived.

Now, with any common sense, one assuredly understands that they picked up some kind of contraband from near the public roads and dropped it off inside the prison Camp compound. Most commonly it's some kind of booze and cigarettes. I've seen them bring in drugs, steaks, and cell phones. Some of these items are simply first-world luxuries that we're deprived of normally and that hold good value for barter in return. With a trained eye, we are able to watch all this happen under the nose of the guards and the people running the prison. We don't get involved in any of this smuggling, and we definitely don't talk about it with other people, especially the authority figures.

Today, to add to our lunchtime entertainment we notice a group from the paint department driving a truck that gets pulled over on this access road by the SIS team. The guards that were recently searching Murillo and I out at the garden are now creeping around this access road and watching the inmates as they cruise around to their work assignments. Many of the inmates are involved in approved work duties. Fixing a fence, delivering food from the warehouse to the compound kitchen, things of this sort. But the paint shop is notorious for getting drugs into the compound lately. Specifically, steroids, Vicodin, and K-2.

We observe it all unfold, like a tsunami that is going to hit land whether you are ready for it or not. The SIS guards are hidden just around a corner in the road and pulling over work trucks at random to search them. Usually, they are simply pulling up on inmates or searching guys who are on foot. Today this hidden checkpoint interrupts the smuggling. Usually, getting caught is averted by pulling the scams while driving an official government-issued vehicle being used for "work purposes."

These poor guys didn't even see it coming. They get stopped and right away our eyes and ears perk up as we watch them get hand-searched and told to sit on the ground as the truck is scoured for anything formidable. Knowing there's a better than sporting chance that they are harboring some sort of unacceptable merchandise, we sit in the cut and observe.

After a short time, we see the grunty correctional officers waving around some items and apparently questioning the inmates. From the looks of it, they found some bottles of Vodka, cell phone chargers, and some porn pics—hundreds of them. There's also some kind of bag containing foodstuff. Probably prime rib, sour cream, or something we don't commonly see in prison. We can't know for sure, but this is entertaining and comical how a simple lunch break grows into a watch party where booze and porn are getting guys thrown into the SHU.

Yes, did I mention that they got put in the Hole? Three inmates, pending further investigation. The SIS team takes their prize catch of the day away to be put under lock and key for an indefinite time period. It may be a week, a month or until they get shipped to another facility, which will take several months.

At the same time, there are other inmates walking past us and we chat for a few minutes here and there. Some make comments on what the paint crew might be getting busted with, while others pay it no mind. Many have seen it all before and are aloof. But be assured, there will be rumors going around by the end of the day about what happened out here at the traffic stop on the service road this afternoon.

A few things are a given in prison: three meals a day, a place to sleep, and a rumor mill that rivals Hollywood, only without the glamour. I'm looking forward to seeing what stories I hear later today about what happened out on the access road. I saw it, so I know what I saw. It will be funny to hear what gets told to me about the event. I almost feel ill at ease with how bored we are and what we do to keep interested inside the institution.

As the incident dies down, our friend Aaron walks up. Great! Our help for the afternoon is starting to arrive. We only have a short time frame (about a week) to handpick the sweet corn when it is at its juicy best. Right now, we are in the heart of that time frame.

Aaron then asks us if we have heard the news. He claims that some guys from the paint department were seen trying to escape in a truck and that they got caught by the FBI down the road off the compound. Amused, I turn to Murillo and we both crack up laughing. In the span of less than 30 minutes the story of the inmates who got carted off to the Hole for contraband has already morphed into a tall tale about an escape that was thwarted by the FBI. How quickly and erroneously news travels in a compressed world.

We all have a good chuckle about truth, reality, and our own impressions of how to deal with living in this place. Murillo claims that this life has never felt real to him. Aaron admits that this place is more like a demented reality show where jokes are always played on us. I state that it reminds me of the movie *The Truman Show*, with Jim Carey. We are the plot, setting, and characters inside this fake little world.

When the rest of our inmate volunteers show up, we all decide to get out into the field and start picking sweet corn. Since the heat of the day is bearing down on us, it's best to get out there and complete as many rows as we can before we overheat or the 4 p.m. count nears.

The next few hours are spent in the field again, this time harvesting the corn by hand. We attach several trailers to the back of the tractor and complete some rows that are each about a third of a mile long. As always, we nibble on some of the fresh corn as we are working, but for the most part we stick to our plan—get a lot done in a short amount of time so the heat doesn't hurt us. Four rows down and four rows back nearly exhaust my fellow workers, so we find the nearest shade to take a break. A productive couple hours of work completed.

As the guys relax with some water, I venture out into the watermelon patch and bring a few ripe ones back for them to munch on. Mind you, all day there has not been a correctional officer overseeing us. Only the visit from the SIS team and the occasional drive by from the head of another department. I tell you this to convey the strange existence we live in at this place.

In the evenings we are locked up in the compound, counted, ordered around like soldiers, and generally bossed by most of the staff. But by day, the select few of us are able to venture out to work at this garden and find our little bit of peace that is otherwise not present during the racket and mayhem that is prison. A strange tug-of-war in our own minds, but we enjoy it.

I theorize that this is why the farmers I work with don't really appreciate what we have out here: they are too new to prison and don't know any better. Again, they are not helping us this afternoon, as they are probably off messing around in the welding shop making tools out of scrap steel. Unnecessarily of course.

We sit for 15 minutes or so in the shade, warm wind rolling over our faces. I learn more about my fellow inmates in the moments of silence out here than in all the forced conversations that happen within the walls of the compound. A few soft discussions take place about women, culture, and family. We all agree that we miss these things the most and find solace in being able to commiserate with like-minded individuals.

There are still a few hours until we have to be back at the compound for 4 p.m. count, so we are breathing in this restful moment in slow motion. A sense of accomplishment and serenity surrounds us. What a worthy feeling to have some tomatoes and corn harvested for our donation to the local churches tomorrow morning. A little good we are still able to offer the world while living in this run-down federal prison. I personally admit to the guys my feelings about our efforts being a penance paid for our wrongs—a way to make things right with society and with God. They agree, and a few of them smile with humble pride.

Just as we were starting to get our fill of the watermelon, we are interrupted by the rumble of two trucks buzzing at a good clip toward us. Turning, we see that they are filled with correctional officers, different than the SIS officers that were patrolling the compound earlier. They pull up near us, but do not exit the vehicles. Rolling down a window, a guard shouts down at us to return to the Camp immediately. There has been an early recall, meaning that something has happened, and they must account for all of us. In this situation, they want our movements controlled and contained.

As inmates, we've learned to take these sorts of situations seriously. No reason to create a stir or complain. We accept that our day in the sun is over, and we gather ourselves together for the half mile walk back to the Camp compound.

Curiosity compels our conversations into predicting what has prompted the authorities to order us all back to the Camp early. It's actually more work for them to orchestrate all of this, so I know that they are not necessarily happy when a recall occurs. The guards must go around and check all the corners of the compound for prisoners, herd us back to our housing units, and then count us when we are there. Then they must deal with whatever situation has prompted this recall, and only the guards that love detective work and doing searches enjoy what goes on now.

Some of the guys think there must have been an attempted escape. Others claim there was probably a fight on the yard. Many of the inmates have been bickering in the housing units, mostly because the cooling system doesn't work, and it has been over 95 degrees for several weeks now. To me, a fight seems logical, I suppose.

I offer up the notion of a drug bust. We've noticed several

groups of guys smuggling in contraband recently and the dudes from the paint shop got caught up earlier today. Surely it must be something along those lines. K-2 is big in prisons these days. It's hard to detect in drug screenings and it is fairly inexpensive compared to other substances. Guys smoke it and get out of their minds. It is an ugly thing to watch, and I don't see the appeal. Nevertheless, it's popular right now and easy to get.

Walking back to the compound, we cross paths with other groups of inmates making their way back to the prison as well. They also offer up their ideas as to what could have happened, spawning stories about busts that have transpired in the past, here and at other penitentiaries. One inmate comments that it's usually a few rogue prisoners that screw things up for the vast majority of the guys doing time in these places. Most of the men, I have come to realize, are just trying to do their time and pass through unscathed so they can get back to their families. A few knuckleheads are always making it harder on us all by hatching some lame-brained scheme and then getting caught. Therefore, any sort of perks that we have, such as TV time or microwave use, are taken away from everyone. The situation we are in today will probably end up no different.

I do hear one fella mention that there were three good 'ol boy farmers who were caught with cell phones in the landscaping department. I dismiss this story as just another rumor and file it with all the other funny speculations we've heard within the last 20 minutes concerning this present recall situation. It would be ironic though, farmers avoiding farm work to go use their smartphones. Cell phones in prison are considered a security risk and can actually get a guy in more trouble than a fist fight. Come to think of it, the farmers are regularly venturing off by themselves, while they also don't necessarily ever care to help me, or be around me for that matter. Curious.

We make it back to the front gate of the Camp and see a line forming. There's a procedural shake down as we enter the compound, where we empty our pockets while getting patted down and wanded with a metal detector, TSA style. This whole process takes almost an hour to get all the inmates rounded up and put back into their respective housing units. We notice the disgust on the guards' faces because of all the extra work they are doing now.

Only one of the guards, a female, is happily doing searches of the inmates. She is enjoying her moment of superiority with her line of questioning and accusations. "Not today gentlemen! No more sexting with your little hussies. Empty your pockets!" It's quite sickening, really, the amount of joy she gets from lording oppression over other humans. There are usually at least a few of the guards working that revel in flinging around their bad attitudes. They will say whatever comes to mind, like a bucket of mud thrown against a wall just to see what sticks. In this case, it was this lady guard who must really hate men, all the while using this situation to unleash her pent-up frustrations.

We file through the line slowly. When my turn arrives, I walk up to the gleeful female, turn around and spread my arms and legs to my sides after emptying my pockets. She must recognize me (I have been at this prison for four years now) because she makes a comment about when I'll finally be leaving this place. I answer her bluntly, "I've got less than a year left here." She continues doing her search and mutters something about public safety and that the community I'll be living in should be nervous. I decide that silence is my ally and complete our time together with tight lips.

Now finished with the scorned guard, I scurry off through the front gate and veer right toward my housing unit. I am reminded several times by guards stationed along the way to go directly to my cell, not stopping, and to prepare for count. Everyone has on their serious face, so I do exactly as they say.

Arriving back in my unit, I see many of the one hundred guys housed there wandering up and down the hall. Each one is proposing what caused this recall. Some are complaining. Others are worried about a large-scale search. Me, I'm just making sure I have enough time to take a quick shower before anything else happens. A peek toward the stalls proves that there is no line and no funny business taking place either. It's always smart to check any questionable areas of the prison before just barging in on something. Drug deal, fist fight, or hanky-panky, a guy doesn't really want to get caught in something that doesn't concern him. It's easy to do if you don't watch yourself in this compressed, cramped environment we live in. Luckily, I've avoided any abrupt, uncomfortable situations by simply being observant.

Freshening up after working outside in the heat is a great feeling, in prison or not. It's rewarding to have worked hard and pleasing to know that I can now slide through the rest of another day. Even though I'm in the shower, I can still hear everything that is going on in the hallway. Conversations, yelling, people pounding on the walls, and just general nonsense. It is best for a guy to learn how to suppress this background noise, although I do overhear something that makes me eavesdrop when I make out what is being said. Again, I hear about some inmates who were caught using cell phones, and there was maybe even an iPad involved as well. Perhaps there is some sort of truth to this story, and I begin to question the integrity of my farmer friends a little more closely.

Suddenly, it all starts to add up. I recall how the farmers regularly want to venture off on their own using some lame baloney excuse. Usually they don't care for my presence, avoiding me if possible. Their stories usually refuse to make sense, but I simply don't mind what they do with their time. I'm always suspicious, though, as to why they don't want to spend more time doing actual farm work since that is their trade of choice in the real world. They were always complaining about me behind my back but would never give me any helpful suggestions to my face. Only smug smiles and "aw shucks" remarks. Well, they had me fooled, but it now looks as if their little antics have caught up to them.

So I ingest these rumors that I overhear once again and wash the soap out of my hair. It takes me a few minutes to dry off and then clothe myself inside the shower stall. I bring some shorts and shoes down to the shower with me so I am somewhat mobile once leaving it. I adopted this practice after watching other guys get hassled when they leave the shower with just a towel wrapped around their waist. With only slick shower shoes as grip, they get pushed around, jabbed at, or even punched since they are in a vulnerable position. Most times it's in jest, but every so often an assault can happen, and leaving the shower unaware can be one of the weakest positions to be in. Thus, I take the extra few minutes to dry off completely and put some clothes and shoes on to venture back to my cell. It isn't the most comfortable practice to put shoes on semi-wet feet, but it beats getting pushed around and your shoes getting taken from you.

So general precautions aside, I make my way back to my bunk where my cellmate is returning from work as well. Charlie is all talk about the early recall, the search upon re-entering the prison, and what incident could have possibly warranted this sort of action. He has a habit of complaining about small things, but with good reason. He has been here for seven years and has three more to do, the epitome of institutionalized. For him, anything that interrupts routine is worthy of slander and cursing.

Charlie inquires if I have seen anything suspicious today or if I know the source of the recall. I must qualify his question because I see suspicious things every day in here. So, I inquire if he means stranger than normal or simply the usual peculiar suspects. We get a good laugh or two as we speculate on what could have happened. We're of the same mindset in that we don't cause a whole lot of trouble nor do we want to. Neither of us get involved with smuggling in contraband, we don't get into fights, nor are we involved with any of the drugs that are circulating this facility.

With this recall, there will be about two hours of downtime where we are stuck in our cells before evening chow is served, so our speculations have us feeling a little put off. It is spurts like this that slow down the days, sitting and waiting for the next opportunity to do something else besides holding down my bunk. It can be a drag—I will never get used to it, but I have learned to endure it.

The guards will circulate through soon, so we both settle down and get ready for a head count. It is during this waiting when I notice something that begins to piece some of the puzzle together even further. One of the farmers lives in a cell across the hall from me. As count is getting ready to begin, everyone is supposed to be in their respective housing units and sequestered into their assigned cells. In preparing for count,

I glance across the hall and notice the farmer isn't present. This quickly leads me to believe that there is some merit in the rumors I've overheard about them getting caught with some unauthorized electronic devices. I mention this to Charlie and his face lights up. Not because he delights in others getting in trouble. No, it's because he loves a good scandal, and this is one he has been predicting for months now.

Charlie has been probing me about these farmers and their honesty. They come off as good 'ol boys, but his intuition seemed to tell him otherwise. Knowing that I work with them, he has been curious as to what they do during the day. He remarks that he spots them drifting around randomly and doesn't think they are as honest as they come off to be. I always stand up for them, but now I'm second guessing my loyalties. Charlie has it figured out and he's probably right, anyhow.

So the guards finally come through for count. When they finish tallying our cell block, they holler to wait patiently by our bunks until evening chow is called. While we wait, Charlie researches his suspicions about the farmers. By talking with many of the guys in our hallway, they all become judge, jury, and executioner with their concocted story. How easily everyone forms their own version of the truth.

Evening chow is an energetic event, so I sit in my bunk to read while waiting to go to eat dinner. I don't mind waiting around for a little while, because the books I've been able to read over the years of being locked up have fully entertained me. Knowing that I will probably not have this much time to read when I get out, I am making the best of my downtime in here. Biographies have become my interest over the past 18 months, and I am engulfed in one about Walt Disney right now that I thoroughly enjoy.

Mr. Disney and I have something in common, only him being on a much grander scale than myself. He always had audacious ideas, and I admired that about him. I, too, had many ambitions in life but often needed others to keep me moving in the right direction. Walt had his brother as the smart businessman to assist him in his endeavors, while I had several friends in my life do the same for me. Ah, the wonders of how life could have been different.

Anyhow, after 20 minutes, I see a crowd of guys congregating around the door that leads out into the main hallway. It must be getting close to dinnertime. Funny thing is, we only know an approximate time they will call chow, but guys get bored and antsy as they chatter and clatter waiting for the dinner bell to ring. The volume increases by the minute, so I find a good place to end my reading for the moment and prepare for the mad dash to the chow hall.

Now, this is another phenomenon that is certainly entertaining to watch. Once chow is called, several hundred inmates rush to the chow hall. There's no shame in it. Some run, some push others out of the way, a few cut in front of guys with wheelchairs and swerve without regard to who is behind them. This is something that only happens here at the Camp. At any other facility of higher security, there would be consequences for inmates acting like this—either from the authorities or from other inmates. Here, though, grown men run wild down the hallway as if the BOP might run out of food this evening.

The first time I witnessed this mad dash, I was concerned. I thought maybe there was a fight, or even a revolt of some sort. It didn't seem violent, just confusing as to what these adults were running toward and why they were in a hurry.

I curiously observed a mob of men, aged 20 to 70, all hurtling themselves toward the chow hall once count was cleared and the dinner bell rang. They resembled a zombie horde, only moving at varying paces and speeds. Many were in the federal issued khakis, while others wore grey sweatpants purchased from the compound commissary. The look on their faces was ravenous and like that of crazy-eyed children. Their mouths were squawking of hunger and complaining of the food even before they had taken their first bite of the evening meal.

The one thing that I realize in how we treat our time here is that nobody is ever in a hurry to do anything. It was recommended to me that the sooner I realize to slow down and go along with this mantra, the easier things would go for me. It is true. Hence, when I see a large group of men running toward the chow hall, I feel cause for concern.

The guards let them get away with this rush to the chow hall here at the Camp in Leavenworth for some reason—laziness and apathy I assume. The COs here at Leavenworth are much more sloth-like than any of the other prisons I have been at. Count is usually a struggle for them, and any efforts beyond those required responsibilities are rare. The guards that work in the evenings aren't like those that work during the day. Once evening chow is called, they usually just sit in the front offices looking at ladies in swimsuits on the internet and smoking on their vape sticks. The inmates, in their mob mentality running to chow, are beyond their care. It's gotten to be quite amusing over the years, if not annoying.

Here's another truth. We can count on three meals a day while in prison. It's a given. It is well known that food is guaranteed to us in here. Everything else is a privilege and can be taken away from us per punishment or behavior modification. We have to wait in line, but the food will be there.

The kitchen staff regularly throws out hundreds of pounds of food following every meal. They make enough food and then throw the leftovers away. This is to make sure that there is no special treatment with inmates getting extra food. Another rule inserted to keep the institution running in a strict and orderly fashion.

So chow is called, men go dashing toward the cafeteria, and another evening is underway. I usually wait for the initial rush to subside and then venture in through the line to dinner. At this evening affair, the guys I know all catch up with each other, and we do our best to conjure up some activities to occupy our time for the next several hours before evening count and lights out at 10 p.m.

Dinner can be a jovial affair with a lot of joking around. Maybe a recap of whatever strange events occurred today or, most often, an exchange of loving taunts that men insult each other with constantly in this place. It's our way of showing love to another guy, to poke fun at him, and bring to light their funny habits and foibles. Anyhow, here we are, in the midst of another evening in the mess hall.

While I am walking to dinner I run across Brad, my friend whom I ran into this morning before work. We are both still eager to play some tennis this evening and agree to meet at the court in about 30 minutes. He tells me that there's a show he wants to watch at 7 p.m. tonight, but we can get in a few sets before then. I smile to myself—tonight should actually be somewhat pleasant with the nice weather, tennis, and a little TV for a nightcap.

The good thing about chow time at a Camp is that the unwritten politics ruling the rest of the prison don't really spill over to how things are handled in here. At other facilities, the inmates are segregated as to where they can sit, who they should associate with, and how they are to maneuver through the dining area. Certain races sit in certain corners of the room. Certain cliques within those races are separated into certain seats, and if you're smart you follow a certain path to your particular seating area. You don't want to amble through the Italians' seating area on the way to sit with your Hispanic buddies—that is considered disrespectful. Use the correct isles and understand the flow of traffic.

Also, you do not want to get caught being cordial with any of the sexual predator criminals, as it will immediately lower your status. You don't want to sit with them, let them walk in front of you, or even acknowledge them, for that matter. Because of this, it's smart to know who everyone is, even if you never really associate with them. Understand what other guys stand for, who the shot-callers are, and who your people are, so you can be around them. These are the people that you can joke around with, sit with, and rely on for your information concerning the rest of the population in here.

Luckily, since getting to the Camp there's not much of this sort of politicking going on during chow time. The rest of Camp life still follows this hierarchy of social activity, but for some reason all bets are off in the chow hall. So you learn how things are, fall in line, and get on to the next thing. The next thing right now is eating and then hustling out to the tennis court for some sets.

I sit with my customary group of guys, and we have the same sort of conversations most every evening. John is there. Aaron too. A few of the other regulars are there, and we all give our account of the farmers getting busted with cell phones and other electronic equipment. I convey my shock in the matter as others proceed to poke fun at my naïveté. I suppose I always just want to expect that people don't lie as much as they really do, especially in here. But as we say, "... it is what it is."

There's the talk of playing tennis this evening as well as an episode *of American Greed* airing at 7 p.m. I wonder if that is what show Brad is eager to see?

We all comment on the quality of the food. Tonight, the kitchen staff has taken chicken and put it though some sort of grinder, like you might do with ground beef. There's some kind of preservative-tasting spice added to it along with a few peppers, onions, and some melted cheese.

The kitchen staff has thrown a hot dog bun on there with some rice and canned green beans to fill up our trays. A plastic spork, thin napkin, and water round out our dinner this evening at Camp Leavenworth. I can't even remember the last time the food from the chow hall didn't taste mechanical. Nonetheless, I remark that it is the best restaurant in town and offer to pick up the tab for the meal this evening. A few groans and smirks arise out of my eating pals, but it is an overused joke that has lost its punch over the years.

We still enjoy each other's company, but don't really stay long. Eat, fast-chat, and move along.

The rest of the inmates in the chow hall have the same thing in mind. Some get in and out of there so they can procure a spot in the exercise area. Others want to get a seat on the benches outside so they can smoke. Smoking is not allowed in federal prison, but it takes place regularly and often in plain sight of the guards.

Chow is also a time where jockeying for position around the Camp takes place. Besides the weight pile and smoking benches, there are nooks around the Camp that are designated for certain groups. Since there's a lot of movement right now, one can see guys checking out guitars to strum and reserving tables in the library for card playing and gambling. Some guys go for walks around the track with headphones in their ears. Others gather to play handball, a popular sport in here.

I have played a fair amount of handball over the years. Now that we have a small group of guys willing to play tennis, my preferences have changed. The tennis court surface is lousy, no doubt. It has cracks all over it causing the ball to take crazy bounces many times during a match. The net is sagging. The surface is loose, causing twisted ankles or sliding on elbows. There's an understood level of danger on this court, but it is ours and we really do enjoy volleying during the summer months.

We check out the rackets from the gym office along with a few used tennis balls. There are only four rackets, and they tell us that no more will be available until next year. This is important because we like playing doubles. Guys playing tennis can often be rough on the equipment and a broken racket isn't unusual. We are down to the final four, so we remind each other to be careful with what little resources we still have. "Don't throw the rackets," we're always asserting to each other.

Tennis ensues and we enjoy the game on the court as well as the banter of wit between men in competition.

After several sets, my partner, Tom (not his real name), and I are winning. He is a banker from Des Moines, Iowa, and only here for about 18 months. He'll leave prison soon, so I will be hunting for a new partner upon his departure. But for today, we play and are enjoying victory.

Next up is Brad and his partner, who we all call Doc. Doc and Brad are also both getting out of prison soon. We enjoy a spirited match over the next hour or so, knowing that this may be one of the last times that we all get to play on this rough court in our little hole we call home for now.

The match ends and we all give up our rackets to another group of guys who want to play this evening as well. Usually, the winner stays on the court until they are beat, similar to basketball pick-up games in parks around the country. However, tonight we all want to get inside to relax in front of the TV for a few hours.

I stick around for another 10 minutes to watch the next group of guys play and quickly notice something different from our competition.

Our previous match was light, jovial, competitive, but with a respectful exchange of attack bouts. This new group of guys that are playing seem to be arguing from the very start of their first set. This makes it awkward to watch. They are also waving their rackets around like swords as if to use them as weapons. I get nervous because I know where this is headed, and it isn't going to end well.

Suddenly, it happened. One guy missed a shot and proceeded to throw his racket onto the ground. The face bent, the strings came loose, and his temper was white hot like the bright sun that waning summer evening.

With the broken racket, so went our doubles tennis playing for the rest of the summer. It's hard to get things in prison. It is even harder to keep the things we do have. Guys in here don't seem to respect what little we have, and it only takes one hothead to make things worse for everyone else. In this case it was one less tennis racket, leaving us with three for the remainder of the summer.

This incident is the beginning of the end for our tennis playing pleasure. As the summer progresses, we still play, but the games start to dwindle along with our interest. I show up less and less because the bad attitudes start to overshadow the fun of the sport. This becomes another lesson to me that in here good things don't really last. It is usually one inmate that messes things up for the rest of the community, and this is just one more example.

Now the time has arrived to head back to the housing unit to freshen up before watching the 7 p.m. airing of *American Greed*. Walking through the hallway reminds me of an open-air market in the Middle East or even lumbering through the stands of a Kansas City Royals game. There is the exchange of goods, being cigarettes and stolen food from the chow hall. Lining the foyers are guys bumming for favors—usually wanting stamps to purchase smokes or drugs. There is the occasional cell phone, although these guys are usually more discreet with their usage. All these things are considered contraband, against the rules of the Bureau, though this does not stop or even curtail their presence.

The hallways are also loud at this time of day. Guys post up in certain areas talking to passersby, holding down their corner, as they do back out on the streets in their own neighborhoods. Many of these guys feel at home here in this place. It doesn't seem to bother them that they are away from society. They still operate as if it's another day on the pavement. I assume their activities are a front. Much of what they do is a façade in here. They feel the need to keep up their status as a lead-role player in this secluded environment.

I ignore most of the chatter, having endured it for several years now. I'm not interested in most of what is going on, anyhow, and don't need any extra black-market chicken that is left over from tonight's meal. I don't smoke or do drugs anymore. I have decided to stay away from cell phones in here as they eventually bring trouble to those involved. There's also no need for me to brag or loudly announce my presence as I make my way down the hall. Any street credit I used to have left me the day I was arrested. So I saunter my way back to my unit minding my own business.

Returning briefly to my cell block, I see Charlie reading in his bunk. This is where one can find him most days at this hour. He is an avid reader, mostly of history or novels involving the Old West. He pops up to chat for a bit, but I make it short, as I want to secure a seat near the TV before it gets too crowded. I tell Charlie what my plans are; otherwise, I may get caught chatting with him for a while. I quickly change clothes and swap a few thoughts with C.W. Mostly we agree that the hallways can be reminiscent of a swap meet or flea market. This is why he spends so much time reading in his bunk, to avoid the annoyances.

It is nearing 7 p.m. so I break away from Charlie and make my way back to the chow hall, which doubles as a TV room when there is no meal going on. Four televisions are posted in different corners of the room that are set to deliver sound out over a predetermined radio channel. This way each inmate can put on his headphones, tune his radio to a particular station, and the sound from the TV is delivered over the individual's radio. It's similar to what has been done in public gyms and other institutions.

The room is already getting crowded, and guys are excited

about tonight's show. Many inmates actually see themselves as celebrities because of their crimes. Most are high profile in their communities since the Feds publicize their trials and convictions. They often involve millions of dollars (as mine did) and bring the attention of the media. When a show's theme is about white-collar criminals and their Ponzi schemes or Chicago drug lords and their hold on a neighborhood, it is something of interest.

I have met many guys who were high profile enough to be mentioned in rap songs or talked about on made-for-TV movies. Tonight, we would watch another episode about some white-collar criminal that heisted millions from the American public. Too many of these guys in here idolize the characters they see on TV. They consider them heroes and cheer with excitement during the shows.

I find my seat while Brad, John, and Aaron all sit nearby. We all quiet down as the episode starts, and I munch on my evening snack of almonds that I toasted in the microwave for a few minutes. This makes them a little snappier—just the way I like them.

As *American Greed* opens, the narrator shares an overview of the episode and, immediately, I am taken aback. One of the first things that appear on the screen is the face of my friend Brad and his family. I quickly come to realize that the episode is about him and the money he embezzled, which is what got him here in federal prison. I'm sure he knew that this episode was going to be about him, but he kept it to himself all day. Little devil!

There's a lot of ranting from the other inmates as they, too, recognize the guy on the screen. I hear some nervous laughter coming from Brad. He isn't completely comfortable with his likeness on the show, and I can understand why. They don't paint the best picture of his activities or character. I suppose that if we are judged by what we do on our worst day that anyone could be considered an asshole. It is certainly evident here. His depiction over the network is slanderous at best.

Regardless, we watch the episode in good spirits with a few jokes throughout. Mostly we take it for what it is, the media's version of his activities during this part of his life. The show unfolds with his family living the jet-set lifestyle. It also portrays him as a conniver, uncaring and selfish. I'm sure there is some truth to all of it. Nonetheless, his life is now front and center for all to judge.

Watching this episode inspires me to contemplate my own situation before coming to prison. At the time, I was making money, spending it, and being quite generous with those around me. Life seemed fun, carefree, and limitless.

This lifestyle also had a dark side. Selfish drives had me making decisions that favored only my temporary needs. Attention from others and trying to please everyone around me were my short-sighted goals. This led to making bad choices, currying favor with the wrong people, losing the respect of those close to me, and ultimately abandoning family and true friends. All at once my feelings start to get the best of me.

Watching *American Greed* tonight gets me more emotional than I want to be in the presence of a hundred other guys, so I get up and head to the bathroom. There I stand in front of the urinal like many times before, and I become depressed. Thinking about why I acted out of character for so many years hurts my head and brings tears to my eyes. My treatment of Emma and my family. Abandoning close friends. Following a poor line of decision-making. I often get frustrated because a

TV show or conversation will affect my mood, being a captive audience, bored and sensory deprived.

So I do the only thing that sets me straight anymore. I pray for forgiveness and for the strength to change things once I finally get out of this place. Having years to wait for an out date and scrutinize all the things that could have been done differently is a mind killer. When I focus on my goals and my place in the universe, it steadies my heart. I can feel the energy begin to return so I can get myself together and prepare to go finish the evening out in the TV room.

This sort of mental hiccup is typical with me. A few times every month for the past five years now I have had these occurrences. It is a grind coming to terms with myself and my circumstances. At this point, I am tired because after so many years of waiting around, there is nothing else to do except endure the suffering. Not being able to take action and make good on all the wrongs committed in the past is a very frustrating spot to be in. Here I am again, this time standing in contemplation.

Flurries of emotions come over me and I strain to keep them in check so that I don't portray weakness in this place. Pushing the emotions back into my stomach, I finish my business and leave the restroom.

The TV show is still unfolding, and the guys are enjoying the portrayal of Brad. Much of the story is the same as he has told us before. At times, we all open up about our pasts and what got us in here. We are somewhat enjoying the fact that Brad is squirming a bit over the media's version of his felonies.

Why is it that as humans we take interest in the folly of others? Because we feel empowered to be in a position of superiority in life's game? I, for one, have been on both sides of the coin. It sure seems like when things are down that they will never pick back up. In relation to that, it also feels like when things are going well that the smooth ride will never end. One thing is for certain about those tables, they always do turn.

I am quiet and contemplative for the rest of the evening. Another episode of *American Greed* is on after Brad's hour-long episode, but it's not as interesting as the one we just watched. We aren't doing time in the same prison as the culprit in this show.

The rest of the prison remains calm for the next several hours. No fights, no yelling or abusive banter. I haven't even seen one of the guards walking around since chow earlier. They stay sequestered up in the front office. It's a pleasant enough evening to burn up the final hours of the day in peace.

When 9:30 p.m. hits, things begin to change. See, we have evening count at 10 p.m. and are locked down for the rest of the evening in our respective dorms until morning count at 5 a.m. is complete. This is part of the institutionalization process that we all adjust to after being in here. It is simply easier to sleep during this lock down and move around when the compound is open to do so. Some guys stay up all night and sleep all day. Each inmate does his time differently; we all get through our sentence in our own way. I never question how another prisoner does his time, so long as it doesn't affect me.

Exuberance picks up over the last 30 minutes before count. A nervous energy spreads through the Camp and the inmates get really hyped up. People are moving through the hallways, talking louder, and making final phone calls to their families before bedding down.

Guys that I don't normally speak with are walking by and making comments about sports or the president or whatever comes to mind. I have realized that they are not trying to initiate conversation, only to blow off the last bit of steam they have built up before the day is over with. One guy I barely know asks if he can borrow two stamps—he wants to get a smoke in before count time. Another tries to tell me that he wishes there were a TV show about his crimes, as if he were proud of them.

It is an interesting phenomenon and can be amusing if you let it. Mostly though, the meaningless jibber-jabber is annoying, just like most of what happens in this place.

I decide to say my goodbyes to the small crowd of associates seated nearby, and I make my way outside for some fresh air before I hit the sack.

The blustery warm evening assaults my unprepared senses. I look around, and the loud chatter out here is similar to inside, but there is also something rather disturbing about 20 feet in front of me. Two inmates are rolling around on the ground in the grass, but they aren't fighting or struggling No, they are high on something called K-2, and this can be a direction the drug takes someone if they are not able to handle the substance.

A few other guys are trying to calm them down and corral them inside—count is coming soon. Several of the inmates are amused at the expense of the drug induced stupor these poor addicts are trapped in. Nonetheless, it seems to be standard operating procedure around this place. When guys get bored, they will search out anything to keep them amused and entertained. It's humiliating, but another reality that I have learned to cope with in here.

Most of the time these K-2 abusers get away with their antics, and the following day we hear stories of the show we missed. Seldom do they get caught, but when they do it's usually a two-week vacation to the SHU before they are released back on compound. Then the cycle starts over. No treatment, no counseling, no help for their disease. Only shame for their weakness. It's an attempt to sweep the problems under a rug instead of dealing with any issues head on. I find this typical of most situations in the BOP, but most of us feel powerless to care, let alone do anything about them. So I do my best to ignore and stay out of the way.

I observe these two inmates squirm around on the ground as they curse, slobber, and yelp like they are having a stroke. One guy's pants are down around his ankles and I believe he shit himself. It's a disaster I just can't turn away from, but I do my best not to stare for longer than a few moments. I feel sorry for these poor souls and pray that they find a better way to live their lives. At least there are a few sober guys around helping them get cleaned up in order to head back to the housing units for count. What a thankless job.

I shake off my disgust and decide my pre-count fresh-air break has found its conclusion. The lingering warm air outside is also another reminder that we need to open the window in our room. The prison is not equipped with air conditioning, and in the heat of summer it can be awfully hard to sleep, what with the humidity, sweat, and overall discomfort. The only parts of the prison that have cool air are the administration offices and guard stations. This also explains why the guards don't venture out from their perch very often.

I return to the main hallway of my housing unit and am happy to kiss another day in this place goodbye. Besides the lively fanfare and elevated noise sparked by anticipation, this is the most pleasant time of the day for me. While others are jumping around like New Year's Eve is just minutes away, I feel a welcome calm. I enjoy my sleep time and especially the dreams that accompany me in this slumber. There is the feeling of accomplishment that another day has been conquered and I am that much closer to going home. The dreams have simply become a mysterious treat over the years of being locked up.

I sit solemnly waiting for count and my cellmate Charlie continues to read in his bunk. He has been stationed there for hours it seems, and he too appreciates the finality of today. We glance at each other and understand that the years in here have proved that patience is an acquired taste. Patience with time itself. Tolerance with other men of all kinds. Serenity in dealing with one's own demons. Your best friend and most heated rival in here are all the same person, the only person that you showed up at this place with. The only person that will leave with you and help you carry on after this stay is long over.

As the hallway outside my room still rings with the noises of fellow inmates preparing for bed, I am grateful that another day is done. I thank the Lord for being with me for one more twenty-four. I pray that my sleep be restful and that my dreams be exciting. I also pray for all of my fellow inmates in here and in prisons around the world. Deep down we know that this is a journey we did not choose, but one that we are on together. We didn't select our traveling companions but are now bonded by concrete and metal. Together we're fused by the ideals that we all brought with us from the first day we showed up in this place. Those plans are to get through this experience the best we can and get back to our lives as soon as we can. In the meantime, we continue on. On to the next thing.

Most of the guys have made it back to their respective rooms by now, and I hear the main door to the housing unit open. A silence falls over the dorm and two correctional officers walk in. The first officer yells out, "COUNT TIME!" Ten p.m. count is here and the official end to my day has arrived. All the inmates stand at attention, facing forward with quiet faces. With as much nonsense that happens around this facility, there is a militaristic silence that occurs right now.

The BOP takes count very seriously, and any interference that occurs during count time can result in disciplinary action. It's an easy problem to avoid and something that inmates choose not to buck. It's just a fight that cannot be won, and so the population of Leavenworth Camp is at attention while count is taking place.

The task is a simple one. The guards must walk up and back down the hallway taking a count of every warm body in attendance. Their count should match the number of inmates assigned to that particular housing unit, and it's usually fairly straightforward. If the count is off, it's a matter of time before the problem is rectified, although this can delay getting to sleep since we must stand until they are able to get the numbers correct.

Fortunately, today is no different. Count is good, lights are turned off, and it is the end to a typical day, incidents notwithstanding.

I briefly chat with Charlie about staying strong and enduring another day. Football season will be here in a few months—another milestone to focus our attention on.

In reality, my mind is poised toward the future. I think about writing this book. I consider what my ex-girlfriend is doing at this very moment. Memories of hanging out on the front porch of my house on the Plaza are still vivid. I miss my family and look forward to the day that they will pick me up and take me away from this place for good.

My eyelids fall over my tired eyes and I know that sleep will be upon me soon. I never have trouble sleeping in this place. Not unless I dwell on how hot it is in here without air conditioning. It was a blazing 99 degrees today and is muggy right now. Not to fear, it's only another uncomfortable issue to deal with while becoming accustomed to prison life. After all, if I wanted things to be comfortable, then I shouldn't have come to prison in the first place.

Learning to farm has become a lifelong skill. The garden project at Leavenworth was a great way for inmates to give back in a productive, meaningful way.

My bunkmate, Charlie, drew this with colored pencil while at Leavenworth. His were just some of the unique skills that I witnessed from guys over the years during my time locked up.

Often times my life felt like a movie, even a cartoon. We all have a story to tell, never neglect to believe that yours is meaningful and with purpose.

REACT

"Tighten your laces. Cut your rations. Keep moving."
—*A Promised Land*, Barack Obama

Choices are part of an equation that became truly remarkable for me as I spent years building my foundation into the person I wanted to be. It starts with our thoughts. Our thoughts lead to our actions. These actions reveal our character. Our character leads us to our destiny. Finally, our desired destiny is to be in harmony with the energy of the universe. How wonderful is it that something so small and within our control can be responsible for something so grand!

By the end of my prison sentence, I was constantly looking for something larger than myself to guide me through each day. Meetings with my case manager were stressful. Determining my actual out date, supervised release plan, job preparations, and when my family would pick me up were just ideas that pinballed in my brain. For years, I had slowed life to a snail's pace to find comfort and get through my years in prison. Decisions were made for me. When to eat, when I could move around, what clothes I could wear. Living in a life of restrictions is oppressive and leaves a person with a yearning for freedom.

Concentrating on a larger purpose than myself kept me humble and calm amidst the constant drag of life. Now, these choices to get my life back in order upon my release were in front of me, and the opportunity to make proper and solid decisions again that would affect my well-being were a welcome boost for a new beginning—small choices to lead me to a remarkable life once again.

Experience can be sinister. Peering into the past, we sometimes wish we had plotted a better course for ourselves. There are too many questions in life to govern our own egos. Maybe if I had stayed with a certain girl when I was younger, we would have beautiful children today. Or should I have taken that regional director promotion instead of quitting for a job at another company? Would I be well off by now and happy in my middle-management American lifestyle? If I had the willpower to stay away from drugs, then would the hardships I went through have been much fewer?

I will never know for sure. Questions and thoughts like these used to haunt me most days. The hours spent in worry outnumbered the hours I was living in the present—in the life that really mattered.

Looking back, I don't think I could have changed the path that I am on now. It was forged for a reason. I may not have liked some of the journey while it was happening, but I made it through stronger and am better off for it.

If I could do it again, would I go about things differently? Damn right I would! I would do it all better because of the wisdom I now have within me. But wisdom doesn't come to a person by wishing it into existence. One must acquire it by the ways and means of the world. A world run by people, fallible people.

Once I accepted that I am a fallible person and will continue to make mistakes going forward, then that is when life started falling into place. It made more sense. We are all just doing the best that we can. Nobody spends a day attempting to fail or disappoint. We simply live the best we know how.

Sometimes the best is not good enough—not up to the standards of others or our own expectations. Either way, many things happen contrary to how we imagine them. If we can accept change, objectivity, humility, responsibility, and then the willingness to do something with ourselves, then we can begin to live our lives to the fullest.

At the heart of it all, our choices define us and our place in eternity. I thought about my own existence for years while locked away. While I earned no college degrees or accolades during this time, I realized the depth and breadth of life in a greater sense than I ever had before. Consider this:

Control can be a major factor to happiness in life. Many of us try to control other people. Some try to control the value of their position at a job. Others love being in control of social groups, whether it be through media or in person. It makes no difference.

The easiest thing to control in life is our own thoughts. We have the power to suppress evil feelings and uplift blissful images. Our mind is able to focus on the positive and avoid negative influences if we so desire. Our decisions shape our existence. Therefore, our lives are within our own control, being sane and solid human beings.

But we are weak. I personally have let outside influences shape my worldview. Other people's opinion of me has helped create my place in the world. This led me to disaster and unhappiness.

Luckily, we have control over this and can change our thoughts at any point in time, starting now. No matter how many undesirable choices we have made in a row, the next choice you make can be honorable. Then the one after that can be noble. Continuing, you can become selfless and worthy of respect by doing the next right thing. Our thoughts, under our own devices, are ours. They're all that we have that is truly our own.

These thoughts lead to our actions in the world. How we carry ourselves. What we do to honor and respect others. Our actions are where we carry out our plans for living and who we choose to follow through on these plans with.

Our thoughts aren't visible to others, but our actions are. These actions are thoughts in motion. It can be a wonderful thing because this is how we begin to interact with the world around us. This is the energy, from our own minds, that we propel out into the sphere in which we live.

As our actions are creating the life we desire for ourselves, others will begin to take notice. They see who we are and form an opinion. The makeup of our character is decided. How we are viewed in the world begins to take shape.

Many people say that we cannot control what others think of us, but I believe this to not be entirely true. We are judged by how we carry ourselves. If our thoughts lead to actions and actions lead to character, then one would presume that our thoughts control how others perceive us.

Now, I'm not innocent enough to suggest that we have control over the thoughts of others. That's nonsense. However, I do offer that if others are forming opinions about our character, then we do have some control over that. By carrying ourselves in righteousness. Through making decisions with love and care toward others. When we think positively, it seeps through all the way to our character. Others will notice this, and they will more clearly see us for who we really are.

The greatest thing about our character is that this is what leads us to our destiny—our place in life and where we want to end up after these years of living. All this time and effort spent on trying to get it right. Should we live for the moment, free-spirited? Is a more deliberate approach the best way to our desired destiny?

I'm not sure. I am only certain that my thoughts now carry through to my actions. My actions are what form my character. This character is what leads me to my destiny, my place in the world. As I dissect life to its simplest state, then this is where I find myself: in control of my thoughts. The willingness to seek truth through my beliefs has all of a sudden led me to a much healthier and happier existence on this planet. All with my eternal focus being on God.

One of the more gratifying lessons that I have finally accepted into my life is that there is always a chance at redemption, no matter how far gone the situation. Regardless of how long it has been or how fruitless it may seem, it is worthwhile to mend bridges and reconnect with people. For me it was a series of bad choices. Maybe more like a ledger full of mistakes because I didn't want to take responsibility for my original mishaps. I wouldn't humble myself to admit mistakes or to right the many wrongs I had succeeded in committing.

This was never more evident than in 2011 when the SWAT

team came through my front door and pulled the proverbial rug out from under me. I had spent the previous several years selling drugs, ignoring my girlfriend, and treating people like pawns in a game of greed. My health was of little concern, proven by the amounts of drugs I did on a daily basis. My loving mother, father, and siblings worried endlessly when they would not hear from me for weeks. Even though life was a mess, I kept running harder and harder to create the illusion that busy meant successful.

Whatever I was attempting to succeed at was fleeting at best.

In the matter of an hour my house, money, and any assets I owned were seized, and I was left to pick up the pieces. I owed money to some people and had nothing to pay with. No cash and nothing to sell to make cash—stuck between the Plaza and Westport. I flailed and faltered, hating every minute of it. Most everyone scattered from my sides. The storm was over, the tornado was gone, and everything around me was in shambles.

Now this is where you might want to hear that I got tough and turned things around, my life spinning back into order. Wrong. I struggled for a while. For years it sucked. There isn't a magic button for redemption. While at the bottom of a pit, the first few steps don't seem so rewarding. But they were the most important.

Whether it was from being scared of going to prison or embarrassed that I was broke, I remember when things started to turn around. It was the day I decided to stop using drugs. To this day, I have not touched any illegal substances after my last go around back in 2012.

When I was broke and scared and losing hope, I was smoking crack. The powder cocaine was not enough anymore, so toward the end I was smoking. When I was high, my mind would completely unfocus and it became easy to forget my dismal existence. My anxiety was on red line all the time, and I was skeptical of almost everyone and everything.

The day I finally stopped was when I listened to what my girlfriend said to me. She had been saying things like this for years, but this day was the day it stuck. I thank God for the courage to hear her that day.

On this particular day, I was planning on going to my girl-friend's house to hang out for the evening. Emma was out running errands, so I had the afternoon to myself before our rendezvous. I had been dealing drugs for years at this point, and I was very adept at doing the drugs myself.

It wasn't often I had much personal time during that stint, so when I was alone, I would consume drugs in bulk for the sake of doing so and for no other reason than that. I had quantities at all times, and it became a duty that I took on for myself. Doing so gave me time to be away from life for a while so I could forget about being me and just be nobody. So for hours before I went over to Emma's, I did drugs and nothing else. Not answering my phone, not making dinner, not reading or doing laundry. Nothing except doing drugs in binge mode. I was smoking crack, measuring out quantities of the drug, moving it around, playing with it, cooking it, and just doing it. All of it. I remember being focused on only one thing and that was to get a better hit than the last one I just did. I was stuck and wanted nothing except to be stuck that day. I was feeling sorry for myself that I had let my life slip away from reality, and escaping it was my only solution.

It seems that this unveiled the mental-health attribute that hindered me. I had such lofty expectations for life, and wallow-ing in my own self-pity was a way of scolding myself for not being good anymore. If I was going to be a subpar person, then

I was going to be the crappiest subpar person there ever was. In my mind, I had given up on any ambitions I had as a kid and this was going to be the last straw that day. I thought the drugs would take over and simply put me to sleep or put me away for good. I didn't know for sure and didn't really have a well-thought-out plan for the afternoon, only that I was doing massive amounts of cocaine for hours by myself and the result would have to speak for itself, whatever that was going to be. So I sat there for hours, not really thinking, just doing with reckless abandon. I kept telling myself that I would make my way over to Emma's house sometime after 7 p.m.

Remembering back to that day is sickening for me. I recall sweating, nose running, eyes bulging, head swirling, and anxiety in overdrive. I would do drugs and then get up and roam around the house. It was sort of a routine to check the front door, feel the windows, peer into the kitchen sink, run water in the bathroom, and then make my way back to the table where I would do more drugs. There was no rationality in it. My mind was racing continuously forward, away from the present. I scurried around the house and then back to the same spot as if to mock myself, running away from my current life and chasing someone who I had once been. But I could not catch up, and my only recourse was to do more drugs and see if that would get me to be a different person.

I had made mistake after mistake in recent years, mostly with the personal relationships in my life that meant anything important. I had alienated the real people in my life, replacing them with dark figures. A few times I considered who I could call for company and comfort. My family was hours away, and the only person who still connected me to the real world was Emma, and she wouldn't be home for several hours yet. So I continued the circuit around my home, smoking crack and nervously fiddling with hardware around my strange house. Time flew by as my mind flew away to somewhere that was out of reach.

I don't remember how, but I did eventually get up and leave my house at some point. The three-block walk over to Emma's place was wobbly and slanted. My mind was a mess; I felt like a drunken ape finding his way through a thick forest. My steps were stuttered and uneven while my breath was short. I was wide awake from the drugs, but my thoughts were cottage cheese, the kind that had been setting in the sun all afternoon. I even grossed myself out knowing that my mouth smelled like burnt glass. I couldn't even drink water without choking. This was a beautiful disaster in tow through the neighborhood streets near the Plaza.

In what seemed like a day and a minute all at once, I made it to the Bradwood Condominiums. I walked in the front door of my girlfriend's place with the composure of a wet cat. I must have looked like chaos, because the minute I walked in she had one word to say to me. That's it. One word. She looked at me with sorry eyes and slowly said, "Reeeaally?" The look of pity stunned me, although I shouldn't have been surprised. I could tell she wanted to do something to help me, but I was the only one that could fix my life that night.

After that, she continued to speak—something about if I was going to be alright and if I had eaten recently. But only that single word was parked in my head. Nothing more. All the problems condensed in my skull were of my own creation, and smoking drugs for hours had spun me to my wits end. But her single expression stuck with me, and the culmination of everything up to that point jarred something loose in my efforts to begin my healing.

That single word didn't sober me up, but that day was the

last time I did drugs. My final party. When she verified how disgusting I had become, I realized that my choices were now limited. The sunset that summer night was my last ray of hope, a final reminder that I couldn't handle this much longer. My body would not be giving me any more chances. I felt the universe speak to me and simply give me a choice. If I wanted the substances that bad, then they were about to win. But if I wanted life, then this was my last warning, and Emma would be the one to nurse me back to health.

Over the years Emma had been opposed to my activities, both business and recreational. She had also spent numerous occasions trying to counsel me back to health or convince me to straighten up. She was tireless in trying to keep me from fading away, but I would never give her the respect she deserved concerning this matter. Only today, one word stood out. Remembering back, I know why that word stood out to me, on that day at that time. It's because I allowed myself to be ready for it. God had been working in me, and that was the spark of return that I needed. My girlfriend was His vessel at that time for me. It was truly a miracle; there is no other way I can accept it. Everything looked different that day at her condo because it was a special moment in time.

I started making small choices that were the building blocks to my foundation. A new foundation that became greater and sturdier than ever before.

Still, things didn't improve much before I went to prison. I didn't leave society in grand style. It was more of a whimper and a sigh. But for about a year before I went to prison, I stayed away from drugs. I began seeking out healthy initiatives, activities, and people. Life didn't seem much better at the time. While this transformation was going on, I was still broke, lonely, and a disappointment to myself and others. But events were unfolding toward a more positive existence.

Sobriety happened. Prison transpired. Spirituality sunk in, and redemption overshadowed everything else. It is still happening every day, right now. It is happening because I allow it. Not because I strive for it. In prayerful meditation, I am able to be at ease with my situation in life, whatever it is currently, and let God do His work. Not me manipulating others or trying to force events into place. No, I am encouraged every day to let rebirth fulfill my destiny in this world.

If I did it all again, would I do it the same? I would certainly say that I'd do it better since I have the experience of success and failure to draw from. Would I sell drugs and surround myself with shady people? Would I take chances in life at the expense of my health, freedom, and relationships? I think most rational people can answer those questions. Plenty of songs are written about wanting to go back and do it all over. But we can't go back.

I lived through all of this and have come out the other side stronger for it. Others need to know that it happened. Things don't have to be hopeless. There are lessons that plenty of people can learn from my former blunders and current triumphs. It is a legacy of erudition, this enlightenment and learning that took place when I was fully unprepared and completely unaware. But God allowed it to happen in me and I gained the insight. The trust. The desire for truth that could not be found in any other form I sought out in this world.

That is what people ought to know. That we will never be right in the world until we allow ourselves the opportunity to know. Be mindful of any and all coincidences throughout your days. See who you interact with because they may lead you toward your true destiny in life. For me it was only one word. The word "Really" delivered by the one closest to me at the time. That one word and the opportunity to listen.

Realize that it is never too late to redeem your former life or achieve one better than your current status. You don't have to be down in the dumps to desire something superior for yourself. Allow it to happen. When you are willing to move on to the next thing in life, then you are allowing yourself to move forward. It isn't a destination, and the ongoing journey is remarkable.

My first run around Kansas City post-prison included this visit to Union Station to ride the new railcar in 2018. So much has changed in my beloved midwest home.

Reconnecting with old friends upon my release gave me a sense of fulfillment back in the world in 2019. From left to right Corbin, Ahren, David, Spencer, Quentin.

TRIUMPH

"In the depth of winter, I finally learned that within me
there lay an invincible summer."
—Albert Camus

*What a crazy time in life, something I had been living toward
for the past 60+ months. I had lost 10 pounds in my final two
weeks in prison, taut like steel rope in a winch. Many guys want
to look better coming out than they did going in. I worked out
like a machine and ate only packets of tuna the month before my
release.*

*Every conversation I had with another inmate was peaceful,
direct, and whether they understood or not, I was telling them
goodbye and good luck in life. The days would still mock me with
their length, boredom, and annoying themes. But not to worry,
the sunrise was on the horizon and life was about to become
bright once again.*

*My release from prison had me feeling like my hair was on fire
for weeks. Out of respect to the guys who still had years to do,
I kept my excitement in check and only spoke of my out-date if
asked about it in casual conversation.*

But it was there in front of me, and I knew walking out of the gate and into the real world was going to be a whack in the face of my institutionalized life.

Those last 24 hours were cathartic. As I cleaned out my locker, I wouldn't be keeping most of the items. Only a few books, letters from over the years, and paperwork would be leaving with me. The things I acquired over the years were simple in nature, but in a place where we have so little, these items have more value than in the real world. A plastic bowl and cup, a few pairs of sweatpants, some decent socks from the commissary, some extra packages of tuna, and even a handful of stamps were all items I would be dispensing to some of my buddies in the unit. They were all super-appreciative, and I was certain not to reveal my glee out of respect.

My final walk around the track out on the yard, the conversations with guys I had spent the past several years doing time with, and even the last time through the chow line were all deliberate and meaningful. I absorbed what had got me here. The patience I learned over the years by being around so many different types of people. The perseverance I formed by keeping my anger in check on days that I felt like running away.

I specifically recall knowing that I could finally live with myself no matter how anxious my life would become. Long suffering had given me an unshakable foundation that I could now be proud of. I didn't feel the same shame in restarting my life at age 40, as I did when this sentence started. The simplicity of life doesn't care about age, only effort and love.

I was carrying two dense packages on the morning I walked out of the prison doors and toward the car full of my crying family. As I lumbered through the parking lot, the doors of my mom's car swung open and a flood of joy sped toward me. Mother, sister, brother, and grandmother all made the trek to Leavenworth, and just like that I was walking outside in freedom. It was all sniffles and yelps while my mom rang a cow bell in the back seat. She was crazy happy, and conversation would have only dulled the moment.

Without looking back, we sped out of the parking lot and away from a place that I never wanted to see again. I didn't even look back; every detail of those buildings will reside with me for the rest of my days. My anxious fingers now fumble on the keyboard as I recall the brick and mortar.

There was a gas station a few blocks away and we decided to stop there so I could buy a drink and a snack and change my clothes into a brand-new colorful outfit that I had specifically requested. Finally, no more khakis. Adidas running pants, blue T-shirt, blue and orange running shoes, and real underwear and socks. In the Quick-Trip restroom, I peered down at the institution clothes I had exited the prison in and let the pile remain on the floor without a second thought. In an instant, I was a citizen again, not a dull-brown-wearing number with the cattle name "inmate." I had comfortable shoes to carry my light body and colorful clothes to brighten the world with.

Exiting the convenience store men's room, I found the isle with the sunflower seeds. It had been since before prison that I had the opportunity to nosh on a bulging mouth of seeds, just like I did when I played baseball as a kid. I stared at the options like an idiot and meekly asked my brother if it was okay that I picked some out. He glared at me and exclaimed, "Dude! Get everything in the store if you wanna!" But I was nervous being out in public and felt like I was doing something wrong; the shock of being scolded for six years straight had its lingering effects.

Suddenly, the universe played another cruel joke on me as a

federal corrections officer waltzed through the entrance of the convenience store. He was clad in the blue button-up shirt with all the insignias and markings of a CO. He had obviously just finished his shift and was stopping for a snack, but the sight of him had me reeling. It took several minutes of me staring at the sunflower seeds to get over the fact that he was not there to take me back to the Camp. I was no longer in their custody, and it was the first reminder of many that my life was burgeoning into new beginnings.

The anxiety would probably be something that I would have to work on to get over. But the meat of my sentence was done, and now it was on to being in the world again. It felt great to be choosing which sunflower seeds to chew on.

###

As I write this, I am 43 years old. I live at my mother's house in a small town in Kansas. This rural setting is regarded as the quintessential place to raise a family and stay safe from crime. I work at a lumberyard and make 10 bucks an hour. Living here allows me to spend my free time catching up with family and old friends. I enjoy doing favors for those around town while reevaluating my future in a more humble setting. Doing a reboot in life, at this age, and in this place, was never a predetermined plan for me ... but I could never be happier.

Ten years ago, I was making 20 grand a week. I was living in a nice part of Kansas City, spending money at a rampant rate and running around without a care in the world. I traveled to Las Vegas, Los Angeles, Chicago, and Phoenix regularly, and must admit that memories of those trips still escape me. I didn't spend time keeping up with anybody I cared about because there were always "more pressing matters" to take care of. I had no concept of the future because living for the moment is all that mattered.

People every day told me that I had it made. They were willing to stick around since I was paying for our daily escapades. From the outside, it would seem that running around casually spending money and partying with whoever was down at the time would be exciting, if not glamorous.

Well, it is tedious and damaging to the soul.

During these haphazard years of coming up in the drug trade, I ignored the signs—the damage that was occurring around me. It's obvious now looking back that the signs were there, but I was eager to stay blind. Who would want to validate themselves if destructive behavior was the common theme? Surrounding myself with untrustworthy people while conducting a daily to-do list consisting of several felonies each day—all while regularly disregarding calls of concern from family and friends. These are simply the easy warning signs that stood out on a regular basis.

I tried to convince myself that I was building something, some sort of criminal business that could actually sustain itself through a downturn in the economy. Truly, I wanted success and for others around me to be successful as well. I desired to one day be able to proclaim, "TRIUMPH!" Alas, the efforts put forth during that time in my life would never achieve those goals. I wondered if that day would ever come.

Well, today is that day. Not because of a booming business I have started or all the accolades I have received over the years. It isn't because of the beautiful family I have raised or charities I have donated to. It is none of those things, because for years I didn't do any of that. Those accomplishments took a back seat to operating a drug habit and an illegal business. I was selfish, and my ship was off course. No, today is that day because I have the chance to start over, with nothing except the love and support of my family and friends. Those people buttressed by a meaningful relationship with God are all that one needs to exclaim, "TRIUMPH!"

It is the feeling you get when a bright sun shines down on your day at the park. It is the hug you get from your mom when she is so glad to have you back home that she cannot speak. It is the excitement you get while staying up late talking with old friends, ignoring the time, your phone, or any other distractions. It is the sense of accomplishment you get from knowing something innately. Now, it is pride I have in overcoming my demons. Going through the shadow of the valley of death and coming out the other side stronger and better. Overcoming not only the heavy use of drugs but also selling them with reckless abandon. Seeing the light of good and knowing that I am back home with all the opportunity in the world to keep moving on to the next right thing.

Triumph now looks like a hug from my niece. It is a high five from my brother because of a great song we just jammed out on the guitar. It is laughter from the other room, mother's heart at ease because all is right in the world again. It is the gaze from an old friend that brings you back 20 years to a gentler time. Often a phone call from my father telling me the view from his Upper East Side apartment is enough for me to smile and look up to the sky in thankful appreciation. Victory today is another chance at being in the real world, leaving all falsehoods and damaging aspirations behind.

You see, we don't have to make all the right choices all the time. All you have to do is the next right thing for your path to stay straight. Today, make the resolution to clearly see the consequences of your choices and decide if you can live with them. Be honest with yourself and know that all the decisions you make have an effect that ripples throughout the rest of society. Of course, the effects are more noticeable immediately around you, and the ripples continue on beyond what you can see and what you may even know. But they are there, and your energy is released into the world for better or for worse.

Consider good choices positive energy that is released into the world, helping to uplift others. When we smile at a stranger, both souls are uplifted. For helping a neighbor, our world is better off. In praising the accomplishments of a co-worker, we are able to revel in the glory of others. While celebrating a holiday with family, we are able to spread love through togetherness and good food! It is the conscious effort placed on these important things in life that can bring triumph back to an ordinary existence.

The bad choices we make are negative energy released into our surroundings. In the grind of daily affirmations, prayers, meditations, and assertions, we can lose focus on the importance of this energy. We can get caught up in what is immediately within our grasp as our world becomes smaller and more self-centered. This is where downfalls can happen—when our eyes turn only inward to our own egos and wants. It's not as if we are trying to be negative with ourselves, but without the consideration of the common good, then we lose sight of the collective consciousness that is our world's aim.

None of these things are new concepts; they were gathered from years of reading and contemplating while waiting around in prison. They are, however, important in understanding the quality of the choices we make every day. Triumph awaits you.

It comes in the form of appreciation and praise of others in your world. When the people around you are fulfilled and joyful, then you in turn can partake in the glory.

The Kansas City Chiefs Super Bowl Parade in early 2020 was sheer joy. This day was one of many blessings I have enjoyed in my new life. From left to right Kristin, Serrell, Corbin.

Friends who supported me through my lowest points in life are irreplaceable. This is one of our last nights out before the pandemic changed social gathering standards nation wide. From left to right Lisa, Corbin, Cristian, Tyler.

THE OTHER SIDE OF THIS

"The leaders who embrace an infinite mindset ...
have the resilience to thrive in an ever-changing world."
—Simon Sinek

Here is the view, plain and simple. Addiction is agony and anxiety sprinkled with a feeling of vacancy in the world. Waking up to a new day doesn't help you understand why it's there or what may have brought on this despair and uncertain strife. You arise harboring pent-up frustration with everything. With yourself, with loved ones, with the anchorman on the news, with sunny weather, with your choice of haircut. If you had to restart every day with no reference to build from, then the unsure schedule of life begins to mount. How could I wake up to worry? It just did not seem right; I couldn't have been born to this planet to suffer.

Mornings were always the worst. It would often take everything I had within me to get through the previous day, and now here I was facing another. Like the slow and steady beat of a marching band back for another trot through a downtown parade. The drummers weren't coming fast, but they weren't stopping either. The bass of the drum and the repetitive rat-a-tat-tat of the day consumed my stomach, then my eyeballs, and finally my skull.

I attempted many methods to try and get myself within the pace of life. There was the straight-edge method where I would only go to work, the gym, and then home to relax and repeat the boring existence. I avoided friends, as they would only want me to leave and go out to eat or maybe even catch a show. That would be too much entertainment and might lead to me desiring a drink and then who knows what substance. In my head, I couldn't handle the fun, so I would spend months at a time avoiding humans and all their raucous living.

There was the juggling method, which I attempted frequently. It seemed the most logical way to live would be to weave in and out of all kinds of lifestyles. Exercise after work sometimes. Maybe on Wednesday I would venture out for a few drinks. Certainly, Friday and Saturday would be full tilt, and I could recover on Sunday if I remembered to do so. Work friends were designated for the weekdays and Plaza friends ruled the weekends. All the while, I was in my head worrying if I was pulling off the work-hard / play-hard lifestyle.

Another method was the activities that put me in federal prison, the one with the most consequences.

Life was draining. I stressed about keeping in touch with people. Old friends, new friends, work acquaintances, business leads, neighbors, the whole lot of them. Why should that be stressful? I worried about ignoring my family too. Immediate family, extended family, family friends. And then the worry turned into a gripping and grinding assault on my personality.

I turned into somebody other than myself, all because I thought I had to please everyone in all walks of life. I was distraught with the idea of going to jail, and the fear of it ruining me was real. A tense, solid rock wall encumbering your brain is no way to proceed throughout the day, but there I was incurring the mental torture of someone who had learned to hate himself. Instead of standing for something, I had fallen for everything.

I was certain that going away for years was going to turn me more into a criminal than a humble, productive citizen in society. Therefore, I was uncertain if I would even make it through my sentence.

It was to the credit of prison that I finally just jumped into the day without hesitation. Time treated you better if you did so and would take the edge off much more obligingly. It took years to fix myself, but I was diligent every day to stick to my simple routine of prayer, meditation, reading helpful books, and conversing with other inmates in a meaningful manner. Listening more than talking helped me the most, and I believe that it helped the other guys who were able to unload their worries on me.

But in addiction, the person inside your skin is questioned constantly. So I finally faced life head on. I peered into a future that I could still be paired with, and I didn't give up. Even in captivity, I was able to find purpose because God was working in me.

Setting little goals throughout each day to get me through to the next was a key component to my survival. These usually centered around each meal and any free time we had afterward. I made sure I got up and ate breakfast every morning. Some guys slept through, but I found it was important to have a civil start. Then, my next goal was to stay busy until lunch. Personal hygiene, reading, performing any work assignment duties, and conversing with my cellie. All these little tasks kept my life moving forward.

This militant organized behavior I had practiced for years carried over to my life after prison and helped me navigate the first few years back in the real world.

I don't know if it was the onset of coronavirus or working in the media for a short time that really changed my worldview. Perspective helps, and going through addiction and prison really made the new challenges in life seem just like a small bump in the road. Now in life, it's just on to the next thing for me. Life is one long infinite journey, and each day when we perpetuate the furtherance of ourselves, it seeps out into the lives of those around us. Seeing how society is dealing with coronavirus really solidified how my "keep on pushing on" attitude is a healthy direction forward.

The addiction I found was not a physical one. I don't really crave drugs anymore, and when I dream of being part of that life, I don't really want any part of it. I don't know how to say that being part of this life, here on our planet at this place and time, isn't really just about the present. It's perplexing, but I realized it is about forever. It's like hopping on a merry-go-round that has already been in motion long before my arrival. I ride temporarily and then depart the ride. But the ride continues and will do so for long after I have walked away. So, what did I do while I was on the ride? Did I enjoy it? Did I waste my time? Did I make a difference, or was I even remembered? It only matters to you, the only one you have to deal with for your whole life. The only way it could matter to others is if it mattered to you.

I am a few years removed from prison now and working with my father who runs a health and longevity clinic in New York. The changes I was able to make in my life during the years of incarceration have helped me aim my efforts toward my father's just cause. Our strive is to help Americans learn to reboot their lives for a longer, more active life well into what most people call retirement. Time is the only asset that matters to me now, and I want to impart this knowledge to as many people who are interested in making the most out of life. Our goal is to help others acquire and spend as much quality time on this planet as possible.

Getting out of prison has not been easy. I have held and lost a few jobs already and still struggle to figure out what motivates people in the world. The 2020 situation changed people and our country, with no sign of return to how things were. But it hasn't bothered me. I learned to roll with the changes and not let things out of my control get the best of me. Armed with this attitude, I cannot see any other way that 2020 should have gone. At least people are taking a step back to assess what is important, finally.

Life will be a struggle, and mental illness is a real thing. I tried all sorts of self-help gimmicks before prison but always fell back into the same bad routines. Simplicity of existence reset my life back to normal, and several years after prison, I handle adversity with candor. Instead of turning to a black-market economy as my crutch, I propel my ideas toward a brighter, ever-growing future.

It came down to two things that I decided to concentrate on when offering the world my gestures of sharing: encouragement and entertainment.

Encouragement to know that up, down, or side-to-side,

we can always be important to this world. I want others to know that wrongs can be righted, mistakes can be fixed, and relationships can be mended. One step at a time.

And also, entertainment—to know that it has been a pleasure to do so. The tales, advice received and given, personal struggles, and specific practices all told to you from my first-hand experiences.

Enjoy all that you do every day in life, especially the difficult times. These times are refining you into what lies thereafter. So the only thing left to do is find the next thing and make sure you get on to it.

*This bulldog named Tooty has been a jewel for my mental health
and for keeping my life in order.*

Taking a moment away from writing to ponder my next move.

BONUS

Excerpt from "Survival on an Island"
Released in October of 2020 amid the height of the coronavirus pandemic.

I Pondered Weak and Weary
By Corbin Bosiljevac

It finally happened, all at once. While it should have been expected, I was not prepared for the adventure of a lifetime that I was about to embark upon. I could never fully be ready for it, but here it was staring me in the face.

Federal prison was my fate.

Looking back, I learned more in those seven years than I ever could have imagined. This was a vacation that I never wanted but was not going to be allowed to miss for anything. To deal with your innermost fears on a daily basis, with nobody to help and no break to gasp for air, should wear a person out. But God never gives you more than you can handle, if you simply trust.

In prison, I experienced the personal growth that I yearned for through college and corporate America. It took adjustments, but the end result is a product of mental stability that I couldn't get through years of strife in the workforce.

The quote, "Fear is the mind killer," as stated clearly in the 1980s sci-fi movie *Dune* is a reality in every facet of life. This is no joke. It paralyzes. It reminds you of how others perceive you and then scoffs while you slump in your own shame. Fear hinders whatever task you attempt, but only until you accept it.

More than anything, it is a device of destruction that causes inaction while missing out on the present, the only thing that is important. Seeing that movie as a kid, this quote stuck with me, as I have fallen victim to fear throughout my life.

Until I experienced the most frightening thing to me, something that I never expected to do, I didn't understand how to live in this world. I only existed in it, but did not LIVE in it. There was a place that not only frightened me; it caused anxiety attacks when faced with its real possibility of becoming my future.

When I was finally led behind locked doors by federal marshals, my world became heavy, and fear collapsed my skull. Five minutes were hours, every nervous twitch and movement was magnified since I was the new guy. Every worldly item was taken from me, and I was no longer able to identify myself by things obtained in life. It was only my character, my poise, and my trust in God that would define me from this point on.

It took a long time in there, years really, to understand my fear of life and to appreciate our place in this world without anxiety. When I finally began to envelope myself into my worry is when I began to finally live. I was 38 years old.

I have written a memoir that chronicles my growth through narratives and anecdotes. It isn't just about the changes; it's about the stories along the way that truly bring humanity to those who struggle.

Fear, it is powerful and paralyzing. It can be a motivator or a handicap. While making you strive, it invariably tears you down, and you are none the wiser.

What I'm saying here is that fear along with truths and uncertainty are the dominating factors in determining where our lives will lead.

So, the best way to deal with fear is to live in it. Just like we must live in the world. Not near it or around it, but IN IT. We can rely on temporary measures to carry us through, but it is our presence that makes our lives real.

I apply this to our current world condition (in 2020) where people are scared because of the coronavirus pandemic. This situation has shaken the country to its core, and it is not only about sickness. It's about jobs, economy, grocery stores, social gatherings, holidays, and our way of life. We are all experiencing first-world problems that are weighing a load on all of us.

Suddenly everything has changed, and the uncertainty has left us all in a different space of understanding. Some are concerned about wearing masks, while others revel in mask ridicule.

Some are still quarantining, while others want to go out into the world and live free, as Americans have known for centuries.

Many Americans are still giving virtual high fives, while others are back to hugging with social distance already the least of their concerns.

Masks, gloves, quarantine, and social distance are all measures that eventually lead to fear. These are temporary solutions for living in the world. Permanent solutions are what we are aiming toward when we refer to "Survival on an Island."

It took time away from society for me to appreciate it and

overcome my worry for the world. Now I am able to view the societal changes of 2020 as simply adjustments to life as we know it.

The part that I am taking more seriously is what is under my control, and that is my health. Specifically, I am focusing on my immune system, cellular makeup, and functionality of my human machine going forward. As long as I do the best I can to keep my biology running optimally, then the constant shifts in the world around me are easier to accept. This certainly keeps my fears subsided realizing that health always comes before money.

About the Author

Corbin Bosiljevac is a product of the midwest. Having graduated from the University of Kansas, he spent most of his adult
life in the Kansas City area. His extensive travels around the U.S.
consisted of outdoor adventure and camping excursions, while
his love for nature endures today. Being able to reform his life
to be health-focused, he now works with his father, Dr. Joseph
Bosiljevac. They operate New York Health and Longevity as
well as Flint Hills Surgical Associates. With the new health
measures put in place during 2020, they focus on immune
boosting therapies and total body rebooting programs.

You can connect with me on:
🌐 https://www.blupressmedia.com
f https://www.facebook.com/Blu-Press-Media-104015661482469

Also by Corbin Bosiljevac

A glimpse into the future of human health, longevity, and immune boosting therapies is the most prudent way to face uncertainty in the world. Our personal health should be the top priority going forward, just as 2020 has shown us. Put your own life into perspective with this matter-of-fact commentary from an NYC surgeon who loves helping people get the most out of life. Go to DrJBoss.com today to learn more about personal health, longevity, and to purchase "Survival on an Island."

Survival on and Island

From the epicenter in NYC, his 2020 journal became the backbone in explaining how Americans felt initially, and what we can do going forward to subside our fears of the world. This was a great project to work on with my father during the onset of the pandemic. With hundreds of natural health tips from a long-time surgeon and many stories pertaining to life's changes, this book was pertinent to its time of release in 2020, and still carries on to this day.